MEDITERRANEAN
DIET COOKBOOK
FOR BEGINNERS

2000 Days of Creative, Healthy, and Nourishing Recipes with an Inspiring 4-Week Meal Plan for Dazzling Flavorful Journeys

by Moira Boyd

"Let's start this journey to embrace the Mediterranean diet, focusing on fresh, wholesome foods that nourish the body and bring joy to every meal!"

Table of Contents

Introduction: What is the Mediterranean Diet?

The Mediterranean diet is a nutritional pattern inspired by the traditional dietary habits of people living in the Mediterranean region, particularly in countries such as Greece, Italy, and Spain. This diet emphasizes consuming **a variety of fresh, whole foods that are rich in nutrients, including vegetables, fruits, whole grains, legumes, nuts, seeds, and healthy fats, primarily from olive oil.** It also includes moderate consumption of fish and poultry, with limited intake of red meat and dairy products.

The Mediterranean diet is not just about food; it also encompasses a lifestyle that includes regular physical activity and enjoying meals with family and friends.

The Mediterranean diet is renowned for its numerous health benefits, which include promoting heart health, supporting weight management, and reducing the risk of chronic diseases such as diabetes and cancer. The diet's focus on whole, minimally processed foods, combined with its balance of macronutrients and antioxidants, contributes to its effectiveness in enhancing overall health and longevity.

Key components of the Mediterranean diet include:

- **Vegetables and Fruits:** Abundant and diverse, they provide essential vitamins, minerals, and antioxidants. Commonly consumed vegetables include tomatoes, cucumbers, spinach, and peppers, while popular fruits are apples, oranges, grapes, and berries.
- **Whole Grains:** Foods like whole wheat, barley, and oats form the foundation of meals, offering fiber and essential nutrients. Whole grain bread and pasta are staples.
- **Legumes and Nuts:** Beans, lentils, almonds, and walnuts are staples, providing protein and healthy fats. These foods are often used in salads, stews, and as snacks.
- **Olive Oil:** The primary source of fat, rich in monounsaturated fats and antioxidants. Olive oil is used for cooking, dressing salads, and drizzling over dishes.
- **Fish and Seafood:** Regular consumption provides omega-3 fatty acids, which are beneficial for heart health. Common choices include salmon, sardines, and shrimp.

- **Moderate Dairy:** Mainly in the form of cheese and yogurt, consumed in moderation. These dairy products are often used in cooking or as part of meals.
- **Herbs and Spices:** Used to flavor food, reducing the need for salt and adding additional health benefits. Popular choices include basil, oregano, rosemary, and garlic.

History and Origins

The roots of **the Mediterranean diet** can be traced back to the traditional eating patterns of people living in the Mediterranean Basin during the mid-20th century. It **gained international recognition in the 1950s**, largely due to the work of American physiologist Ancel Keys. Keys conducted the Seven Countries Study, which compared the dietary habits of different populations and found that those following a Mediterranean diet had significantly lower rates of heart disease compared to those consuming a typical Western diet.

The traditional Mediterranean diet reflects the culinary customs of regions like Crete, Southern Italy, and mainland Greece.

These areas were characterized by limited economic resources but abundant natural produce. The diet naturally evolved to emphasize **locally available, seasonal foods, which were simple to prepare and rich in nutrients**.

In these communities, meals were not just about sustenance but were integral to social and cultural life. Families and friends gathered to share meals, which fostered a sense of community and well-being. This social aspect of dining is a crucial component of the Mediterranean diet, contributing to its overall health benefits.

The Mediterranean Diet Pyramid is a nutrition guide that was developed by the Oldways Preservation Trust, the Harvard School of Public Health, and the World Health Organization in 1993.
It summarizes the Mediterranean Diet pattern of eating, suggesting the types and frequency of foods that should be enjoyed every day.

Harvard food pyramid for the Mediterranean Diet. Author: EAT, DRINK, AND BE HEALTHY by Walter C. Willett, M.D. Source: https://en.wikipedia.org/wiki/Mediterranean_Diet_Pyramid

Core Principles and Philosophy

The Mediterranean diet is not merely a way of eating; it is a holistic lifestyle approach that encompasses various aspects of daily life. Here are the core principles:

1. Plant-Based Foods: The foundation of the diet is built on vegetables, fruits, whole grains, legumes, nuts, and seeds. These foods are nutrient-dense and provide essential vitamins, minerals, and fiber.

2. Healthy Fats: Olive oil is the primary source of fat, known for its monounsaturated fats that support heart health. Nuts and seeds also contribute beneficial fats.

3. Moderate Protein: Fish and seafood are preferred sources of protein, consumed at least twice a week. Poultry and eggs are included in moderation, while red meat is limited.

4. Dairy: Cheese and yogurt are consumed in moderation, providing calcium and probiotics.

5. Flavor with Herbs and Spices: Meals are flavored with herbs and spices instead of salt, enhancing taste and offering additional health benefits.

6. Red Wine: Consumed in moderation, typically one glass per day for women and up to two for men, often with meals.

7. Physical Activity: Regular physical activity is encouraged, aligning with the active lifestyles traditionally seen in Mediterranean communities.

8. Social Connections: Meals are often shared with family and friends, emphasizing the social and cultural importance of eating together.

9. Mindful Eating: The diet encourages mindful eating, enjoying meals without rush, and focusing on the quality of food rather than the quantity.

By adhering to these principles, the Mediterranean diet promotes overall well-being, longevity, and a reduced risk of chronic diseases. This book aims to provide you with a collection of easy-to-prepare, delicious Mediterranean recipes that fit seamlessly into your busy lifestyle, allowing you to embrace this healthy and enjoyable way of eating.

I'm Moira Boyd. With my professional background in nutrition and dietetics, and extensive experience in culinary arts, I have dedicated my career to promoting healthy eating habits.

My passion for the Mediterranean diet stems from its proven health benefits and the joy it brings to the dining table. Having traveled extensively through the Mediterranean region, I have had the privilege of learning authentic recipes and cooking techniques from local chefs and home cooks.

As a nutritionist, I understand how vital a proper diet is for maintaining health and preventing chronic diseases. I'm excited to guide you through each recipe and tip, designed to make adopting the Mediterranean diet straightforward and enjoyable. My goal is to help you live a richer, more active life through food that not only fuels but heals. I'm thrilled to share these insights and recipes with you, aiming to make your daily routine both healthier and more enjoyable.

By the end of this book, not only will you have a repertoire of wonderful recipes, you'll also have a deeper understanding of how to embrace the Mediterranean lifestyle and live vibrantly.

Let's begin this journey together with the first chapter, setting the foundation for a healthier, more enjoyable way of eating. Prepare to transform how you eat, feel, and enjoy life, one meal at a time.

Chapter 1: A Guide to Delicious and Nutritious Recipes

Delicious, nutritious recipes are the heart of a successful diabetic diet. This chapter provides a wide range of recipes for every meal, ensuring variety and satisfaction. Whether you are looking for quick breakfasts, satisfying lunches, hearty dinners, or tasty snacks and desserts, you'll find something to suit your taste and nutritional needs.

Maximizing Your Recipe Experience
Each recipe in this book is crafted to highlight the rich flavors of the Mediterranean diet. Here's how to make the most out of these recipes:

Mediterranean Recipe

Note: *The portion sizes and number of servings in these Mediterranean diet recipes are approximate. Adjust the portions based on the number of people to ensure everyone enjoys the meal.*

The words "tablespoon" and "teaspoon" have been shortened to "tbsp" and "tsp".

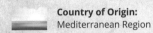
Country of Origin:
Mediterranean Region

Country of Origin:

This section highlights the region or country where the dish is traditionally believed to have originated. Please note that this information is approximate and is meant to provide a general cultural and historical context for the recipe. It does not claim absolute accuracy, as the true origins of many dishes can be difficult to pinpoint precisely.

Prep: Varies | **Cook:** Varies | **Total:** Varies | **Level:** Varies | **Serves:** Varies

| Prep: 5 mins | Cook: 5 mins | Total: 10 mins | Level: 2/5 | Servings: 1 |

Ingredients: Use fresh, high-quality ingredients for the best flavor and nutritional value. Mediterranean cooking emphasizes seasonal produce, whole grains, and lean proteins.

Preparation: Before you begin, make sure you have all the necessary ingredients and equipment. Some recipes may require marinating or other advance preparation.

Cooking Tips: Pay attention to any specific tips or techniques mentioned in the recipe to achieve the desired outcome.

Serving Suggestions: Many recipes include ideas for pairing with other dishes or adding garnishes to enhance the presentation and flavor.

Chef's Tips:

- *The Chef's Tips section contains unique nuances that will help make your dish even more delicious. Use fresh herbs instead of dried ones for a more vibrant flavor. Prepare your own spice blends tailored to your taste preferences. Adding a touch of high-quality extra virgin olive oil at the end of cooking can enhance richness and depth. Experiment with freshly squeezed lemon juice to add a burst of freshness to your dishes. Also, don't be afraid to adjust seasonings to suit your palate.*

Nutritional Values:

- This section provides essential information about the nutritional content of each recipe, including the amount of calories, carbohydrates, protein, fat, cholesterol, sodium, fiber, and sugars. Understanding these values can help you make informed choices to meet your dietary needs and health goals.

Interesting Fact:

- In this section of each recipe, we provide a unique and captivating tidbit about the dish's history, nutritional benefits, culinary tips, ingredient origins, serving traditions, or fun facts to enrich your cooking experience and connect you with the rich heritage of Mediterranean cuisine.

Enhancing Your Mediterranean Diet Experience

Here are some tips on how you can maximize these recipes and adopt a Mediterranean lifestyle:

- **Experiment with Flavors:** Don't be afraid to adjust seasonings or try new herbs and spices to suit your taste preferences.
- **Incorporate Variety:** The Mediterranean diet is all about diversity. Rotate through different recipes to enjoy a wide range of nutrients and flavors.
- **Mindful Eating:** Take the time to savor each meal, focusing on the textures and flavors. Eating slowly and mindfully is an integral part of the Mediterranean approach to food.
- **Pair with Physical Activity:** Complement your healthy eating habits with regular physical activity, another cornerstone of the Mediterranean lifestyle.

Embracing Mediterranean-Style Living

This book is more than just a collection of recipes; it's an invitation to embrace the Mediterranean lifestyle, renowned for its focus on health and well-being. Here's how you can incorporate these principles into your daily life:

- **Savoring Meals with Others:** Enjoy meals with family and friends to cultivate a sense of community and deepen your connections.
- **Balancing Your Plate:** Strive for a balanced diet by including a variety of food groups, with an emphasis on whole, minimally processed foods typical of the Mediterranean diet.
- **Listening to Your Body:** Be mindful of your body's hunger and fullness signals, eating when you're hungry and stopping when you're satisfied.

By following the guidance in this book and integrating the Mediterranean diet into your daily routine, you'll experience delicious meals that are not only delightful to your taste buds but also beneficial for your health. Gather fresh ingredients and embark on a culinary journey to explore the rich and healthy heritage of Mediterranean cuisine, one flavorful dish at a time.

START YOUR DAY RIGHT

QUICK AND NUTRITIOUS MEDITERRANEAN BREAKFAST RECIPES

01 Bruschetta

Country of Origin: Italy

Prep: 10 mins | **Cook:** 5 mins | **Total:** 15 mins | **Level:** 1/5 | **Servings:** 1

Ingredients

- Chicken breasts: 2 (200g each, 7.05 oz each),
- Olive oil: 2 tbsp (30 ml, 1.01 oz),
- Lemon juice: 2 tbsp (30 ml, 1.01 oz),
- Fresh thyme: 2 tsp, chopped (4g, 0.14 oz),
- Garlic: 2 cloves, minced,
- Salt and pepper: to taste,
- Lemon slices: for garnish

Instructions

- **Preparation:** Toast the slices of whole grain bread until crispy.
- **Assembly:** In a bowl, combine cherry tomatoes, fresh basil, minced garlic, extra virgin olive oil, balsamic vinegar, salt, and black pepper. Mix well to combine all ingredients.
- **Serving:** Spoon the tomato mixture evenly over the toasted bread slices. Top with crumbled feta cheese. Serve immediately, enjoying the fresh and vibrant flavors of the Mediterranean.

 Interesting Fact: Bruschetta, originating from Italy, dates back to the 15th century. It was originally a way to salvage stale bread by adding olive oil, garlic, and tomatoes, transforming it into a delicious and satisfying meal.

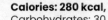

Calories: 280 kcal,
Carbohydrates: 30 g, Protein: 8 g, Fat: 14 g (Saturated Fat: 3 g, Monounsaturated Fat: 8 g, Polyunsaturated Fat: 1 g), Cholesterol: 10 mg, Sodium: 400 mg, Fiber: 5 g, Sugars: 6g

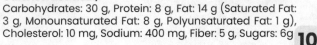

 Chef's Tips: "For an extra burst of flavor, rub the toasted bread with a cut garlic clove before adding the tomato mixture. You can also drizzle some extra balsamic vinegar on top for a tangy kick."

02 Oatmeal with Fruits and Seeds

Country of Origin:
Mediterranean Region

 Prep: 5 mins | **Cook:** 10 mins | **Total:** 15 mins | **Level:** 2/5 | **Servings:** 1

Ingredients

- Rolled oats: 1 cup (90g, 3.17 oz),
- Water or milk: 2 cups (475ml, 16.6 oz),
- Apple: 1, chopped (150g, 5.29 oz),
- Chia seeds: 1 tbsp (12g, 0.42 oz),
- Flaxseeds: 1 tbsp (10g, 0.35 oz),
- Fresh berries (optional): a handful (50g, 1.76 oz)

Instructions

- **Preparation:** Chop the apple into small pieces.
- **Cooking:** Bring water or milk to a boil in a pot. Add oats and reduce heat to simmer, cooking for about 5 minutes, stirring occasionally. Add chopped apple, chia seeds, and flaxseeds, cooking for another 2-3 minutes until the oats are tender and the mixture thickens.
- **Assembly:** Serve the oatmeal in a bowl, topped with fresh berries if desired.

- **Serving:** Serve hot, drizzled with a bit of honey or maple syrup for added sweetness. Enjoy this hearty breakfast with a side of freshly brewed coffee or a glass of orange juice.

 Calories: 320 kcal,
Carbohydrates: 55 g, Protein: 8 g, Fat: 8 g (Saturated Fat: 1 g, Monounsaturated Fat: 2 g, Polyunsaturated Fat: 4 g), Cholesterol: 0 mg, Sodium: 10 mg, Fiber: 10 g, Sugars: 15 g

 Interesting Fact: Oatmeal has been a breakfast, valued for its heart-healthy benefits and versatility.

 Chef's Tips: "Sprinkle cinnamon or nutmeg on top for extra flavor. Try different fruits like bananas or pears."

03 Avocado Toast with Poached Egg

Country of Origin:
Spain

 Prep: 5 mins | **Cook:** 5 mins | **Total:** 10 mins | **Level:** 2/5 | **Servings:** 1

Ingredients

- Whole grain bread: 1 slice (30g, 1.06 oz),
- Ripe avocado: 1 (150g, 5.29 oz),
- Egg: 1 (50g, 1.76 oz),
- Salt and pepper: to taste, Lemon juice: a squeeze

Instructions

- **Preparation:** Toast the bread. Peel, pit, and mash the avocado, seasoning with salt, pepper, and a squeeze of lemon juice.
- **Cooking:** Bring water to a simmer (around 85°C/185°F). Crack the egg into a cup, and gently lower it into the simmering water. Poach for 3-4 minutes.
- **Assembly:** Spread mashed avocado on the toast. Top with the poached egg and season with additional salt and pepper if desired.
- **Serving:** Garnish with fresh herbs like parsley or chives. Serve immediately with a side of mixed greens dressed with olive oil and balsamic vinegar for a complete meal. Pair with a cup of your favorite herbal tea or a fresh smoothie.

 Calories: 290 kcal,
Carbohydrates: 19 g, Protein: 13 g, Fat: 20g (Saturated Fat: 4g, Monounsaturated Fat: 10g, Polyunsaturated Fat: 3 g), Cholesterol: 185 mg, Sodium: 360 mg, Fiber: 7 g, Sugars: 2 g

 Interesting Fact: Avocado toast has gained popularity worldwide as a nutritious breakfast option, combining the healthy fats of avocado with the protein of a poached egg.

 Chef's Tips: "Add red pepper flakes to the avocado for a spicy kick."

04 Blueberry Smoothie with Almonds

Country of Origin: Mediterranean Region

Prep: 5 mins | **Cook:** 0 mins | **Total:** 5 mins | **Level:** 1/5 | **Servings:** 1

Ingredients

- Fresh blueberries: 1 cup (150g, 5.3 oz),
- Greek yogurt: 1/2 cup (120g, 4.2 oz),
- Almond milk: 1 cup (240ml, 8.1 oz),
- Honey: 1 tbsp (21g, 0.74 oz),
- Almonds: 2 tbsp (30g, 1.06 oz),
- Ice cubes: 1 cup (240ml, 8.1 oz)

 Calories: 280 kcal,
Carbohydrates: 38 g, Protein: 10 g, Fat: 10 g (Saturated Fat: 1 g, Monounsaturated Fat: 6 g, Polyunsaturated Fat: 2 g), Cholesterol: 5 mg, Sodium: 90 mg, Fiber: 5 g, Sugars: 28 g

 Interesting Fact: Blueberries are known for their high antioxidant content, which can help fight inflammation and improve brain health.

 Chef's Tips: "For a thicker smoothie, add a frozen banana. For extra flavor, add a pinch of cinnamon or vanilla extract."

Instructions

- **Preparation:** Rinse the blueberries. Roughly chop the almonds.
- **Blending:** In a blender, combine blueberries, Greek yogurt, almond milk, honey, and ice cubes. Blend until smooth.
- **Assembly:** Pour the smoothie into a glass.
- **Serving:** Serve immediately, topped with chopped almonds for added crunch.

05 Tomato and Spinach Omelette

Country of Origin: Spain

Prep: 10 mins | **Cook:** 15 mins | **Total:** 25 mins | **Level:** 3/5 | **Servings:** 2

Ingredients

- Eggs: 3 large (150g, 5.3 oz),
- Spinach: 1 cup (30g, 1 oz),
- Tomatoes: 1 medium (120g, 4.2 oz),
- Olive oil: 1 tbsp (15ml, 0.5 oz),
- Salt and pepper to taste

 Calories: 250 kcal,
Carbohydrates: 6 g, Protein: 18 g, Fat: 18 g (Saturated Fat: 4 g, Monounsaturated Fat: 10 g, Polyunsaturated Fat: 2 g), Cholesterol: 375 mg, Sodium: 220 mg, Fiber: 2 g, Sugars: 3 g

 Interesting Fact: Omelettes are a versatile dish found in many Mediterranean cuisines, often enjoyed for breakfast or a light meal.

Chef's Tips: "For a fluffier omelette, add a splash of milk or water to the beaten eggs before cooking. You can also add other vegetables like mushrooms or bell peppers for more variety."

Instructions

- **Preparation:** Beat the eggs in a bowl and season with salt and pepper. Chop the spinach and tomatoes.
- **Cooking:** Heat olive oil in a non-stick pan over medium heat. Add spinach and tomatoes, cook for 2-3 minutes until softened. Pour in the beaten eggs.
- **Assembly:** Cook the omelette for about 5 minutes, gently lifting the edges to allow the uncooked egg to flow underneath. Fold the omelette in half.
- **Serving:** Serve hot, garnished with a sprinkle of fresh herbs like parsley or chives.

Oat Pancakes with Berries

Country of Origin: Mediterranean Region

 Prep: 10 mins | **Cook:** 10 mins | **Total:** 20 mins | **Level:** 2/5 | **Servings:** 2

Ingredients

- Rolled oats: 1 cup (90g, 3.17 oz),
- Milk: 1 cup (240ml, 8.12 oz),
- Egg: 1 (50g, 1.76 oz),
- Baking powder: 1 tsp (4g, 0.14 oz),
- Honey: 1 tbsp (21g, 0.74 oz),
- Vanilla extract: 1 tsp (5ml, 0.17 oz),
- Mixed berries: 1 cup (150g, 5.29 oz),
- Olive oil: 1 tbsp (15ml, 0.51 oz),
- Greek yogurt: for serving (optional)

Instructions

- **Preparation:** Blend rolled oats in a blender until they become a fine powder. In a bowl, mix the oat flour, milk, egg, baking powder, honey, and vanilla extract until smooth.
- **Cooking:** Heat olive oil in a non-stick skillet over medium heat. Pour small amounts of batter into the skillet to form pancakes. Cook for 2-3 minutes on each side until golden brown.

- **Assembly:** Stack the pancakes on a plate.
- **Serving:** Top with mixed berries and a dollop of Greek yogurt if desired. Serve immediately.

 Calories: 300 kcal,
Carbohydrates: 45 g, Protein: 10 g, Fat: 10 g (Saturated Fat: 2 g, Monounsaturated Fat: 5 g, Polyunsaturated Fat: 1 g), Cholesterol: 55 mg, Sodium: 200 mg, Fiber: 6 g, Sugars: 15g

 Interesting Fact: Oat pancakes are a healthy twist on traditional pancakes, offering a good source of fiber and protein to start your day.

 Chef's Tips: "For extra flavor, add a pinch of cinnamon to the batter. You can also use almond or soy milk for a dairy-free option."

Eggs with Vegetables and Cheese

Country of Origin: Greece

 Prep: 5 mins |  **Cook:** 10 mins | **Total:** 15 mins | **Level:** 2/5 | **Servings:** 2

Ingredients

- Eggs: 4 (200g, 7.05 oz),
- Bell pepper: 1, diced (120g, 4.23 oz),
- Tomato: 1, diced (150g, 5.29 oz),
- Spinach: 1 cup (30g, 1.06 oz),
- Olive oil: 2 tbsp (30ml, 1.01 oz),
- Feta cheese: 4 tbsp, crumbled (60g, 2.12 oz),
- Salt and pepper: to taste

Instructions

- **Preparation:** Wash and dice the bell pepper and tomato. Chop the spinach if necessary.
- **Cooking:** Heat olive oil in a skillet over medium heat. Add bell pepper and cook for 3-4 minutes until softened. Add tomato and spinach, cook until spinach is wilted. Beat eggs, season with salt and pepper, and pour into skillet. Cook until eggs are set, stirring occasionally. Sprinkle feta cheese on top.
- **Assembly:** Ensure the eggs are evenly cooked and the cheese is slightly melted.
- **Serving:** Serve hot, garnished with fresh herbs like parsley or basil. Enjoy this flavorful breakfast with a slice of whole grain toast.

 Calories: 200 kcal,
Carbs: 5 g, Protein: 14 g, Fat: 14 g (Saturated Fat: 3 g, Monounsaturated Fat: 8 g, Polyunsaturated Fat: 2 g), Cholesterol: 370 mg, Sodium: 300 mg, Fiber: 1 g, Sugars: 3 g

 Interesting Fact: Eggs are a versatile ingredient in Greek cuisine, often combined with fresh vegetables and herbs for a nutritious and satisfying meal.

 Chef's Tips: "For extra flavor, add a pinch of smoked paprika."

Banana Yogurt Pancakes

08

Country of Origin: Mediterranean Region

 Prep: 10 mins | **Cook:** 10 mins | **Total:** 20 mins | **Level:** 2/5 | **Servings:** 2

Ingredients

- Whole wheat flour: 1 cup (120g, 4.23 oz),
- Baking powder: 1 tsp (4g, 0.14 oz),
- Salt: a pinch,
- Greek yogurt: 1 cup (245g, 8.64 oz),
- Egg: 1 (50g, 1.76 oz),
- Milk: 1/2 cup (120ml, 4.23 oz),
- Banana: 1, mashed (120g, 4.23 oz),
- Honey: 1 tbsp (21g, 0.74 oz),
- Olive oil: 1 tbsp (15ml, 0.51 oz)

 Calories: 300 kcal,
Carbohydrates: 45 g, Protein: 10 g, Fat: 10 g (Saturated Fat: 2 g, Monounsaturated Fat: 5 g, Polyunsaturated Fat: 1 g), Cholesterol: 55 mg, Sodium: 200 mg, Fiber: 5 g, Sugars: 15 g

 Interesting Fact: Banana yogurt pancakes are a modern twist on traditional pancakes, combining the natural sweetness of bananas with the protein and probiotics from Greek yogurt.

 Chef's Tips: "For extra flavor, add a dash of cinnamon or nutmeg to the batter. You can also add chopped nuts or chocolate chips for variation."

Instructions

- **Preparation:** In a bowl, mix whole wheat flour, baking powder, and a pinch of salt. In another bowl, whisk together Greek yogurt, egg, milk, mashed banana, and honey. Combine the wet and dry ingredients, stirring until smooth.
- **Cooking:** Heat olive oil in a non-stick skillet over medium heat. Pour small amounts of batter into the skillet to form pancakes. Cook for 2-3 minutes on each side until golden brown.
- **Assembly:** Stack the pancakes on a plate.
- **Serving:** Serve warm, topped with extra banana slices and a drizzle of honey. Enjoy with a side of fresh berries or a dollop of Greek yogurt.

Fruit Salad with Honey and Nuts

09

Country of Origin: Mediterranean Region

 Prep: 10 mins | **Cook:** 0 mins | **Total:** 10 mins | **Level:** 1/5 | **Servings:** 2

Ingredients

- Mixed fruits (strawberries, blueberries, kiwi, apple, banana): 2 cups (300g, 10.58 oz),
- Honey: 2 tbsp (42g, 1.48 oz),
- Chopped nuts (walnuts, almonds): 2 tbsp (30g, 1.06 oz),
- Fresh mint: for garnish

Instructions

- **Preparation:** Wash and chop the mixed fruits into bite-sized pieces.
- **Assembly:** In a large bowl, combine the chopped fruits. Drizzle honey over the fruits and gently toss to combine.
- **Serving:** Sprinkle chopped nuts on top and garnish with fresh mint leaves. Serve immediately.

 Calories: 200 kcal,
Carbohydrates: 40 g, Protein: 3 g, Fat: 5 g (Saturated Fat: 0.5 g, Monounsaturated Fat: 2 g, Polyunsaturated Fat: 2 g), Cholesterol: 0 mg, Sodium: 10 mg, Fiber: 7g, Sugars: 30 g

Interesting Fact: Fruit salads are commonly enjoyed in Mediterranean countries as a light breakfast.

Chef's Tips: "For added flavor, squeeze a bit of lemon or lime juice over the fruit salad. You can also add a dollop of Greek yogurt for extra creaminess."

10 Avocado and Tomato Toasts

 Country of Origin: Spain

Prep: 5 mins | **Cook:** 5 mins | **Total:** 10 mins | **Level:** 1/5 | **Servings:** 2

Ingredients

- Whole grain bread: 2 slices (60g, 2.12 oz),
- Ripe avocado: 1 (150g, 5.29 oz),
- Tomato: 1, sliced (150g, 5.29 oz),
- Olive oil: 1 tbsp (15ml, 0.51 oz),
- Salt and pepper: to taste,
- Lemon juice: a squeeze

Instructions

- **Preparation:** Toast the bread slices.
- **Assembly:** Peel, pit, and mash the avocado, seasoning with salt, pepper, and a squeeze of lemon juice. Spread mashed avocado on the toasted bread. Top with tomato slices.
- **Serving:** Drizzle with olive oil and season with additional salt and pepper if desired. Serve immediately.

 Calories: 150 kcal, Carbohydrates: 35 g, Protein: 2 g, Fat: 2 g (Saturated Fat: 0 g, Monounsaturated Fat: 0.5 g, Polyunsaturated Fat: 0.5 g), Cholesterol: 0 mg, Sodium: 60 mg, Fiber: 4 g, Sugars: 19 g

 Interesting Fact: Avocado toast is popular in Spain, celebrated for its combination of healthy fats, fiber, and fresh flavors.

 Chef's Tips: "For added nutrition, include a tablespoon of flax seeds or a handful of spinach."

11 Green Fruit Smoothie

 Country of Origin: Mediterranean Region

Prep: 5 mins | **Cook:** 0 mins | **Total:** 5 mins | **Level:** 1/5 | **Servings:** 2

Ingredients

- Spinach: 1 cup (30g, 1.06 oz),
- Kale: 1 cup (30g, 1.06 oz),
- Banana: 1 (120g, 4.23 oz),
- Green apple: 1, chopped (150g, 5.29 oz),
- Almond milk: 1 cup (240ml, 8.12 oz),
- Honey: 1 tbsp (21g, 0.74 oz),
- Lemon juice: 1 tbsp (15ml, 0.51 oz)

Instructions

- **Preparation:** Chop the green apple and banana.
- **Cooking:** Combine all ingredients in a blender. Blend until smooth.
- **Assembly:** Pour into glasses.
- **Serving:** Serve immediately.

 Chef's Tips: "Add a handful of mint leaves for a refreshing twist. You can also use kale instead of spinach."

 Calories: 200 kcal, Carbohydrates: 40 g, Protein: 6 g, Fat: 3 g (Saturated Fat: 1 g, Monounsaturated Fat: 1 g, Polyunsaturated Fat: 0.5 g), Cholesterol: 5 mg, Sodium: 70 mg, Fiber: 5 g, Sugars: 30 g

 Interesting Fact: Green smoothies are a nutritious way to incorporate leafy greens into your diet, providing a boost of vitamins and antioxidants.

12 Yogurt with Granola and Berries

 Country of Origin:
Greece

 Prep: 5 mins | **Cook:** 0 mins | **Total:** 5 mins | **Level:** 1/5 | **Servings:** 2

Ingredients

- Greek yogurt: 1 cup (245g, 8.64 oz),
- Granola: 1/2 cup (60g, 2.12 oz),
- Mixed berries (strawberries, blueberries, raspberries): 1 cup (150g, 5.29 oz),
- Honey: 2 tbsp (42g, 1.48 oz)

Instructions

- **Preparation:** Spoon Greek yogurt into bowls.
- **Assembly:** Top yogurt with granola and mixed berries.
- **Serving:** Drizzle with honey. Serve immediately.

 Chef's Tips: "For extra crunch, add a handful of chopped nuts. You can also mix in a tablespoon of chia seeds for added nutrition."

 Calories: 300 kcal,
Carbohydrates: 45 g, Protein: 10 g, Fat: 10 g (Saturated Fat: 3 g, Monounsaturated Fat: 4 g, Polyunsaturated Fat: 2 g), Cholesterol: 10 mg, Sodium: 100 mg, Fiber: 5 g, Sugars: 25 g

 Interesting Fact: Combining yogurt with granola and berries makes for a balanced breakfast rich in probiotics, fiber, and antioxidants.

13 Mushroom Spinach Omelette

Country of Origin:
Spain

 **Prep:** 5 mins | **Cook:** 10 mins | **Total:** 15 mins | **Level:** 2/5 | **Servings:** 2

Ingredients

- Eggs: 4 (200g, 7.05 oz),
- Fresh spinach: 1 cup (30g, 1.06 oz),
- Mushrooms: 1 cup, sliced (100g, 3.52 oz),
- Olive oil: 2 tbsp (30ml, 1.01 oz),
- Garlic: 1 clove, minced (3g, 0.11 oz),
- Salt and pepper: to taste,
- Feta cheese: 4 tbsp, crumbled (60g, 2.12 oz)

Instructions

- **Preparation:** Wash and chop the spinach. Slice the mushrooms. Mince the garlic.
- **Cooking:** Heat olive oil in a non-stick skillet over medium heat. Add mushrooms and cook until softened. Add spinach and arlic, cooking until spinach is wilted. Beat eggs, season with salt and pepper, and pour into skillet. Cook until eggs are set, about 5 minutes. Sprinkle feta cheese
- **Assembly:** Ensure the omelette is evenly cooked and the cheese is slightly melted.
- **Serving:** Serve hot, garnished with fresh herbs such as parsley or chives. Enjoy this savory breakfast with a slice of whole grain toast.

 Calories: 400 kcal,
Carbohydrates: 10 g, Protein: 30 g, Fat: 28 g (Saturated Fat: 8 g, Monounsaturated Fat: 14 g, Polyunsaturated Fat: 3 g), Cholesterol: 744 mg, Sodium: 800 mg, Fiber: 4 g, Sugars: 4g

 Interesting Fact: In Spain, omelettes are often referred to as "tortillas" and are a staple in Spanish cuisine, typically made with a variety of fresh ingredients like vegetables and cheese.

 Chef's Tips: "For added flavor, include a splash of vanilla extract or a few fresh mint leaves."

Couscous with Vegetables and Hummus

Country of Origin: North Africa

 Prep: 10 mins | Cook: 5 mins | Total: 15 mins | Level: 1/5 | Servings: 1

Ingredients

- Couscous: 1/2 cup, uncooked (90g, 3.17 oz),
- Cherry tomatoes: 1/4 cup, halved (45g, 1.6 oz),
- Cucumber: 1/4 cup, diced (30g, 1.06 oz),
- Red bell pepper: 1/4 cup, diced (30g, 1.06 oz),
- Red onion: 2 tbsp, finely chopped (15g, 0.53 oz),
- Fresh parsley: 1 tbsp, chopped (5g, 0.18 oz),
- Hummus: 2 tbsp (30g, 1.06 oz),
- Lemon juice: 1 tbsp (15g, 0.53 oz),
- Extra virgin olive oil: 1 tbsp (14g, 0.5 oz),
- Salt: to taste, Black pepper: to taste

Instructions

- **Preparation:** Cook the couscous according to package instructions and let it cool. Halve the cherry tomatoes, dice the cucumber and red bell pepper, and finely chop the red onion.
- **Assembly:** In a large bowl, combine the cooked couscous, cherry tomatoes, cucumber, red bell pepper, red onion, and fresh parsley. Add lemon juice and olive oil, then season with salt and black pepper. Mix well.
- **Serving:** ransfer the couscous salad to a serving plate. Add a dollop of hummus on the side or on top. Serve immediately, enjoying a refreshing and flavorful Mediterranean breakfast.

 Calories: 320 kcal,
Carbohydrates: 45 g, Protein: 8 g, Fat: 12 g (Saturated Fat: 2 g, Monounsaturated Fat: 8 g, Polyunsaturated Fat: 2 g), Cholesterol: 0 mg, Sodium: 300 mg, Fiber: 7 g, Sugars: 6 g

 Interesting Fact: Couscous is a traditional North African dish made from steamed semolina wheat. It has been a staple in Mediterranean cuisine for centuries due to its quick cooking time and versatility in various dishes.

 Chef's Tips: "This dish is great for meal prep; you can make it ahead of time and store it in the fridge for up to 2 days."

Greek Yogurt and Berry Smoothie

Country of Origin: Mediterranean Region

 Prep: 5 mins | Cook: 0 mins | Total: 5 mins | Level: 1/5 | Servings: 2

Ingredients

- Mixed berries (e.g., strawberries, blueberries, raspberries): 2 cups (300g, 10.58 oz),
- Banana: 1 (120g, 4.23 oz),
- Greek yogurt: 1 cup (245g, 8.64 oz),
- Honey: 2 tbsp (42g, 1.48 oz),
- Almond milk: 1 cup (240ml, 8.12 oz),
- Ice cubes: 1 cup (240ml, 8.12 oz)

Instructions

- **Preparation:** Wash the mixed berries and peel the banana.
- **Assembly:** Combine mixed berries, banana, Greek yogurt, honey, almond milk, and ice cubes in a blender.
- **Serving:** Blend until smooth. Pour into glasses and serve immediately.

 Chef's Tips: "For added nutrition, include a handful of spinach or a tablespoon of chia seeds."

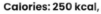 **Calories: 250 kcal,**
Carbohydrates: 45 g, Protein: 8 g, Fat: 5 g (Saturated Fat: 2g, Monounsaturated Fat: 1 g, Polyunsaturated Fat: 0.5 g), Cholesterol: 10 mg, Sodium: 60 mg, Fiber: 8 g, Sugars: 35 g

 Interesting Fact: Smoothies are a quick way to enjoy the nutritional benefits of fruits and yogurt, making them popular for breakfast or a healthy snack.

16 Soft-Boiled Eggs with Greens

 Country of Origin: Greece

 Prep: 5 mins | **Cook:** 5 mins | **Total:** 10 mins | **Level:** 1/5 | **Servings:** 2

Ingredients

- Eggs: 4 (200g, 7.05 oz),
- Fresh spinach: 2 cups (60g, 2.12 oz),
- Olive oil: 1 tbsp (15ml, 0.51 oz),
- Salt and pepper: to taste,
- Lemon juice: a squeeze

 Calories: 150 kcal,
Carbohydrates: 2 g, Protein: 12 g, Fat: 10 g (Saturated Fat: 2 g, Monounsaturated Fat: 5 g, Polyunsaturated Fat: 1 g), Cholesterol: 372 mg, Sodium: 250 mg, Fiber: 1 g, Sugars: 1 g

 Interesting Fact: Soft-boiled eggs are a popular breakfast in Greece, often served with a variety of sautéed greens for a nutritious start to the day.

 Chef's Tips: "For added flavor, sprinkle some crumbled feta cheese or chopped herbs like parsley or chives."

Instructions

- **Preparation:** Bring a pot of water to a boil. Add the eggs and cook for 5-6 minutes for soft-boiled eggs. Meanwhile, wash the spinach.
- **Assembly:** Heat olive oil in a skillet over medium heat. Add spinach and sauté until wilted, about 2-3 minutes. Season with salt, pepper, and a squeeze of lemon juice.
- **Serving:** Place the sautéed spinach on plates. Peel the soft-boiled eggs and place them on top of the spinach. Season with additional salt and pepper if desired.

17 Fruits with Yogurt

 Country of Origin: Greece

 Prep: 5 mins | **Cook:** 0 mins | **Total:** 5 mins | **Level:** 1/5 | **Servings:** 2

Ingredients

- Greek yogurt: 2 cups (490g, 17.28 oz),
- Mixed fresh fruits (e.g., berries, apple, banana): 2 cups (300g, 10.58 oz),
- Honey: 2 tbsp (42g, 1.48 oz),
- Granola: 1/2 cup (60g, 2.12 oz)

Instructions

- **Preparation:** Wash and chop the mixed fresh fruits into bite-sized pieces.
- **Assembly:** In two bowls, evenly distribute the Greek yogurt, mixed fresh fruits, and granola.
- **Serving:** Drizzle honey over the top. Serve immediately.

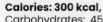 **Calories: 300 kcal,**
Carbohydrates: 45 g, Protein: 10 g, Fat: 8g (Saturated Fat: 3g, Monounsaturated Fat: 3g, Polyunsaturated Fat: 2 g), Cholesterol: 10 mg, Sodium: 70 mg, Fiber: 5 g, Sugars: 30g

 Interesting Fact: In Greece, yogurt with honey and fruits is a common breakfast or dessert, appreciated for its simplicity and nutritional balance.

 Chef's Tips: "Add a sprinkle of cinnamon or a handful of nuts for extra crunch."

Mediterranean Scrambled Eggs with Feta and Spinach

Country of Origin: Greece

 Prep: 5 mins | **Cook:** 10 mins | **Total:** 15 mins | **Level:** 1/5 | **Servings:** 2

Ingredients

- Eggs: 4 (200g, 7.05 oz),
- Fresh spinach: 2 cups (60g, 2.12 oz),
- Feta cheese: 1/4 cup, crumbled (60g, 2.12 oz),
- Olive oil: 1 tbsp (15ml, 0.5 oz),
- Cherry tomatoes: 1/2 cup, halved (80g, 2.82 oz),
- Salt and pepper: to taste,
- Fresh parsley: for garnish

Instructions

- **Preparation:** Crack the eggs into a bowl, whisk with salt and pepper. Rinse and halve the cherry tomatoes, crumble the feta.
- **Cooking:** Heat olive oil in a skillet over medium heat. Add spinach, cook until wilted (2-3 min). Pour in eggs, cook for 30 seconds, stir. When almost set, add tomatoes and feta, cook until set but moist.

- **Serving:** Divide scrambled eggs between plates. Garnish with parsley. Serve hot with whole grain toast or fresh fruit salad.

 Calories: 250 kcal,
Carbohydrates: 6 g, Protein: 18 g, Fat: 17 g (Saturated Fat: 6g, Monounsaturated Fat: 8 g, Polyunsaturated Fat: 1g), Cholesterol: 380 mg, Sodium: 430 mg, Fiber: 2g, Sugars: 3 g

 Interesting Fact: Spinach is rich in iron and vitamins A and C, while feta cheese adds a tangy flavor and has been a staple in Greek cuisine for thousands of years.

 Chef's Tips: "Use fresh spinach for best flavor. Add a pinch of dried oregano or a splash of lemon juice for extra taste."

Protein Pancakes with Berries

Country of Origin: Mediterranean Region

 Prep: 10 mins | **Cook:** 10 mins | **Total:** 20 mins | **Level:** 2/5 | **Servings:** 2

Ingredients

- Rolled oats: 1 cup (90g, 3.17 oz),
- Cottage cheese: 1/2 cup (115g, 4.06 oz),
- Eggs: 2 (100g, 3.52 oz),
- Baking powder: 1 tsp (4g, 0.14 oz),
- Vanilla extract: 1 tsp (5ml, 0.17 oz),
- Mixed berries: 1 cup (150g, 5.29 oz),
- Olive oil: 1 tbsp (15ml, 0.51 oz),
- Greek yogurt: for serving (optional)

Instructions

- **Preparation:** Blend the rolled oats in a blender until they become a fine powder. In a bowl, mix the oat flour, cottage cheese, eggs, baking powder, and vanilla extract until smooth.
- **Cooking:** Heat olive oil in a non-stick skillet over medium heat. Pour small amounts of batter into the skillet to form pancakes. Cook for 2-3 minutes on each side until golden brown.
- **Assembly:** Stack the pancakes on a plate.
- **Serving:** Top with mixed berries and a dollop of Greek yogurt if desired. Serve immediately.

 Chef's Tips: "For extra flavor, add a pinch of cinnamon to the batter. You can also use almond or soy milk for a dairy-free option."

 Calories: 320 kcal,
Carbohydrates: 45 g, Protein: 15 g, Fat: 12 g (Saturated Fat: 3 g, Monounsaturated Fat: 5 g, Polyunsaturated Fat: 2 g), Cholesterol: 185 mg, Sodium: 300mg, Fiber: 6g, Sugars: 10 g

 Interesting Fact: Protein pancakes offer higher protein content, supporting muscle maintenance and energy.

20 Chia Seed Pudding with Mango

Country of Origin:
Mediterranean Region

Prep: 10 mins | **Cook:** 0 mins | **Total:** 10 mins +chilling | **Level:** 1/5 | **Servings:** 2

Ingredients

- Chia seeds: 1/4 cup (40g, 1.41 oz),
- Almond milk: 1 cup (240ml, 8.12 oz),
- Honey: 1 tbsp (21g, 0.74 oz),
- Vanilla extract: 1 tsp (5ml, 0.17 oz),
- Mango: 1, diced (200g, 7.05 oz),
- Fresh mint: for garnish

Calories: 220 kcal,
Carbohydrates: 30 g, Protein: 6 g, Fat: 9g (Saturated Fat: 1g, Monounsaturated Fat: 2 g, Polyunsaturated Fat: 6 g), Cholesterol: 0 mg, Sodium: 60 mg, Fiber: 10 g, Sugars: 20 g

Interesting Fact: Chia seed pudding, inspired by Mediterranean dietary practices, is rich in fiber and omega-3 fatty acids, making it a nutritious choice for breakfast or dessert.

Chef's Tips: "For a creamier texture, use coconut milk instead of almond milk."

Instructions

- **Preparation:** In a bowl, combine chia seeds, almond milk, honey, and vanilla extract. Stir well.
- **Cooking:** Refrigerate the mixture for at least 2 hours or overnight, stirring occasionally to prevent clumping.
- **Assembly:** Once the pudding has set, divide it into serving bowls. Top with diced mango.
- **Serving:** Garnish with fresh mint leaves. Serve chilled.

21 Shakshuka

Country of Origin:
North Africa

Prep: 10 mins | **Cook:** 15 mins | **Total:** 25 mins | **Level:** 3/5 | **Servings:** 2

Ingredients

- Olive oil: 2 tbsp (30ml, 1.01 oz), O
- nion: 1, chopped (150g, 5.29 oz),
- Bell pepper: 1, chopped (120g, 4.23 oz),
- Garlic cloves: 3, minced (9g, 0.32 oz),
- Tomatoes: 4, chopped (400g, 14.1 oz),
- Tomato paste: 2 tbsp (30g, 1.06 oz), C
- umin: 1 tsp (2g, 0.07 oz),
- Paprika: 1 tsp (2g, 0.07 oz),
- Chili powder: 1/2 tsp (1g, 0.03 oz),
- Salt and pepper: to taste,
- Eggs: 4 (200g, 7.05 oz),
- Fresh parsley: for garnish

Calories: 300 kcal,
Carbs: 20 g, Protein: 12 g, Fat: 20 g (Sat. Fat: 4 g, Mono. Fat: 12 g, Poly. Fat: 2 g), Cholesterol: 372 mg, Sodium: 450 mg, Fiber: 6 g, Sugars: 10 g

Interesting Fact: Shakshuka, a traditional North African dish, is especially popular in Tunisia and is now a beloved Mediterranean breakfast.

Chef's Tips: "Add sugar if tomatoes are acidic. Increase chili powder for spiciness."

Instructions

- **Preparation:** Chop onion, bell pepper, and tomatoes. Mince garlic.
- **Cooking:** Heat oil in a skillet. Sauté onion and bell pepper for 5 min. Add garlic, cook for 1 min. Stir in tomatoes, paste, cumin, paprika, chili powder, salt, and pepper. Cook for 5 min. Make wells in sauce, crack eggs into wells, cover, and cook for 5 min.
- **Assembly:** Ensure eggs are cooked. Adjust seasoning.
- **Serving:** Garnish with parsley. Serve with crusty bread or pita.

POWER YOUR DAY

22 Pasta with Vegetables and Olive Oil

Country of Origin: Italy

Prep: 10 mins | **Cook:** 15 mins | **Total:** 25 mins | **Level:** 3/5 | **Servings:** 2

Calories: 400 kcal,
Carbohydrates: 60 g, Protein: 10 g, Fat: 15 g (Saturated Fat: 2 g, Monounsaturated Fat: 10 g, Polyunsaturated Fat: 2 g), Cholesterol: 0 mg, Sodium: 150 mg, Fiber: 8 g, Sugars: 10 g

Interesting Fact: Pasta with vegetables is a traditional Italian dish that showcases the use of fresh, seasonal produce.

Chef's Tips: "Add a sprinkle of Parmesan cheese for extra flavor."

Ingredients

- Whole grain pasta: 200g (7.05 oz),
- Mixed vegetables (e.g., zucchini, red bell peppers, cherry tomatoes): 2 cups (300g, 10.58 oz),
- Olive oil: 2 tbsp (30ml, 1.01 oz),
- Garlic: 2 cloves, minced (6g, 0.21 oz),
- Fresh basil: for garnish,
- Salt and pepper: to taste

Instructions

- **Preparation:** Cook pasta according to package instructions. Chop vegetables and mince garlic.
- **Cooking:** Heat olive oil in a skillet. Sauté garlic for 1 min, add vegetables, cook until tender, about 10 min.
- **Assembly:** Toss cooked pasta with vegetables in the skillet. Season with salt and pepper.
- **Serving:** Garnish with fresh basil and serve hot.

23 Grilled Fish with Lemon and Herbs

Country of Origin: Greece

Prep: 10 mins | **Cook:** 15 mins | **Total:** 25 mins | **Level:** 3/5 | **Servings:** 2

Ingredients

- White fish fillets (e.g., cod, halibut): 2 (300g, 10.58 oz),
- Olive oil: 2 tbsp (30ml, 1.01 oz),
- Lemon: 1, sliced (100g, 3.53 oz),
- Fresh herbs (e.g., thyme, rosemary): 2 tbsp (10g, 0.35 oz),
- Salt and pepper: to taste

Instructions

- **Preparation:** Preheat grill to medium-high. Brush fish with olive oil, season with salt, pepper, and herbs.
- **Cooking:** Grill fish for 4-5 min per side, or until cooked through. Grill lemon slices for 1-2 min.
- **Assembly:** Plate the fish and top with grilled lemon slices.
- **Serving:** Garnish with extra herbs and serve immediately.

Calories: 250 kcal,
Carbohydrates: 5 g, Protein: 25 g, Fat: 15 g (Saturated Fat: 2 g, Monounsaturated Fat: 10 g, Polyunsaturated Fat: 2 g), Cholesterol: 70 mg, Sodium: 200 mg, Fiber: 1 g, Sugars: 1 g

Interesting Fact: Grilling fish with lemon and herbs is a staple in Greek cuisine, highlighting the fresh flavors of the Mediterranean.

Chef's Tips: "Serve with a side of grilled vegetables or a fresh salad."

24 Chicken Fillet with Tomatoes and Basil
Country of Origin: Italy

Prep: 10 mins | **Cook:** 20 mins | **Total:** 30 mins | **Level:** 2/5 | **Servings:** 2

Ingredients

- Chicken breast fillets: 2 (300g, 10.58 oz),
- Olive oil: 2 tbsp (30ml, 1.01 oz),
- Cherry tomatoes: 1 cup (150g, 5.29 oz),
- Fresh basil: 1/4 cup (10g, 0.35 oz),
- Garlic: 2 cloves, minced (6g, 0.21 oz),
- Salt and pepper: to taste

Instructions

- **Preparation:** Season chicken with salt and pepper. Halve cherry tomatoes and chop basil.
- **Cooking:** Heat olive oil in a skillet over medium heat. Cook chicken fillets for 5-7 min per side. Add garlic, cook for 1 min. Add cherry tomatoes, cook until soft, about 5min.
- **Assembly:** Top chicken with tomatoes and basil.
- **Serving:** Serve hot, garnished with additional basil leaves.

Chef's Tips: "For extra flavor, add a splash of balsamic vinegar when cooking the tomatoes."

Calories: 350 kcal,
Carbohydrates: 6 g, Protein: 35 g, Fat: 20 g (Saturated Fat: 3 g, Monounsaturated Fat: 12 g, Polyunsaturated Fat: 2 g), Cholesterol: 100 mg, Sodium: 400 mg, Fiber: 2g, Sugars: 4 g

Interesting Fact: This dish is a classic Italian recipe that highlights the fresh flavors of tomatoes and basil, a popular combination in Mediterranean cuisine.

25 Couscous with Vegetables and Spices

Country of Origin: Morocco

 Prep: 10 mins | **Cook:** 15 mins | **Total:** 25 mins | **Level:** 2/5 | **Servings:** 2

Ingredients

- Couscous: 1 cup (180g, 6.34 oz),
- Olive oil: 2 tbsp (30ml, 1.01 oz),
- Onion: 1, chopped (150g, 5.29 oz),
- Carrot: 1, diced (70g, 2.47 oz),
- Zucchini: 1, diced (150g, 5.29 oz),
- Bell pepper: 1, chopped (120g, 4.23 oz),
- Chickpeas: 1 cup (240g, 8.47 oz),
- Vegetable broth: 1 cup (240ml, 8.12 oz),
- Cumin: 1 tsp (2g, 0.07 oz),
- Paprika: 1 tsp (2g, 0.07 oz),
- Turmeric: 1/2 tsp (1g, 0.03oz),
- Salt and pepper: to taste,
- Fresh parsley: for garnish

Instructions

- **Preparation:** Chop the onion, carrot, zucchini, and bell pepper. Rinse and drain the chickpeas.
- **Cooking:** Heat olive oil in a large skillet over medium heat. Sauté onion until translucent, about 3 min. Add carrot, zucchini, bell pepper, cumin, paprika, and turmeric. Cook for 5 min. Add chickpeas and vegetable broth, bring to a boil. Stir in couscous, cover, and remove from heat. Let sit for 5 min.
- **Assembly:** Fluff couscous with a fork and mix with vegetables.
- **Serving:** Garnish with fresh parsley and serve hot.

 Calories: 400 kcal,
Carbohydrates: 70 g, Protein: 10 g, Fat: 10 g (Saturated Fat: 1.5 g, Monounsaturated Fat: 6 g, Polyunsaturated Fat: 1 g), Cholesterol: 0 mg, Sodium: 400 mg, Fiber: 10 g, Sugars: 10 g

 Interesting Fact: Couscous is a staple in Moroccan cuisine, traditionally steamed and served with a variety of vegetables and spices.

 Chef's Tips: "Add raisins or dried apricots for a touch of sweetness."

26 Stuffed Peppers with Rice and Vegetables

Country of Origin: Mediterranean Region

 Prep: 15 mins | **Cook:** 45 mins |  **Total:** 60 mins | **Level:** 3/5 | **Servings:** 2

Ingredients

- Red or yellow Bell peppers: 2 (240g, 8.47 oz),
- Cooked rice: 1/2 cup (90g, 3.17 oz),
- Olive oil: 1 tbsp (15ml, 0.51 oz),
- Onion: 1/2, chopped (75g, 2.65 oz),
- Carrot: 1/2, diced (35g, 1.23 oz),
- Zucchini: 1/2, diced (75g, 2.65 oz),
- Garlic: 1 clove, minced (3g, 0.11 oz),
- Canned tomatoes: 1/2 cup (120g, 4.23 oz),
- Fresh parsley: 2 tbsp (5g, 0.18 oz),
- Salt and pepper: to taste,
- Vegetable broth: 1/2 cup (120ml, 4.06 oz)

Instructions

- **Preparation:** Preheat the oven to 375ºF (190ºC). Cut tops off bell peppers and remove seeds. Chop onion, carrot, zucchini, and garlic.
- **Cooking:** Heat olive oil in a skillet. Sauté onion, carrot, zucchini, and garlic for 5 min. Add rice, tomatoes, parsley, salt, and pepper. Mix well.
- **Assembly:** Stuff peppers with the mixture. Place in a baking dish, pour broth around, cover with foil.
- **Serving:** Bake for 35-40 min, until tender. Garnish with parsley, serve hot.

 Chef's Tips: "Add grated cheese on top before baking for extra flavor."

 Calories: Calories: 250 kcal,
Carbohydrates: 40 g, Protein: 5 g, Fat: 10 g (Saturated Fat: 1.5 g, Monounsaturated Fat: 6 g, Polyunsaturated Fat: 1 g), Cholesterol: 0 mg, Sodium: 350 mg, Fiber: 5 g, Sugars: 8 g

 Interesting Fact: Stuffed peppers are popular throughout the Mediterranean, with variations reflecting local traditions and seasonal vegetables.

27 Lemon Herb Salmon

 Country of Origin: Greece

 Prep: 10 mins | **Cook:** 15 mins | **Total:** 25 mins | **Level:** 2/5 | **Servings:** 2

Ingredients

- Salmon fillets: 2 (300g, 10.58 oz),
- Olive oil: 2 tbsp (30ml, 1.01 oz),
- Lemon: 1, sliced (100g, 3.53 oz),
- Fresh herbs (e.g., thyme, rosemary, dill): 2 tbsp (10g, 0.35 oz),
- Garlic: 2 cloves, minced (6g, 0.21 oz),
- Salt and pepper: to taste

Instructions

- **Preparation:** Preheat the oven to 375ºF (190ºC). Season salmon with salt, pepper, minced garlic, and fresh herbs.
- **Cooking:** Heat olive oil in an oven-safe skillet over medium heat. Sear salmon fillets for 2-3 min per side. Add lemon slices on top of salmon. Transfer skillet to oven, bake for 10-12 min.
- **Assembly:** Plate the salmon, drizzle with pan juices.
- **Serving:** Garnish with additional herbs and serve with a side of steamed vegetables or a fresh salad.

 Calories: 350 kcal,
Carbohydrates: 5 g, Protein: 25 g, Fat: 25 g (Saturated Fat: 4 g, Monounsaturated Fat: 14 g, Polyunsaturated Fat: 6 g), Cholesterol: 70 mg, Sodium: 150 mg, Fiber: 1 g, Sugars: 1 g

 Interesting Fact: Lemon herb salmon is a classic Greek dish that highlights the use of fresh herbs and citrus to enhance the natural flavors of the fish.

 Chef's Tips: "For a more intense flavor, marinate the salmon with herbs and lemon for 30 min before cooking."

28 Tuna and Bean Salad

 **Country of Origin:** Mediterranean Region

 Prep: 10 mins | **Cook:** 0 mins | **Total:** 10 mins | **Level:** 1/5 | **Servings:** 2

Ingredients

- Canned tuna: 1 can (150g, 5.29 oz),
- Cannellini beans: 1 can (240g, 8.47 oz), drained and rinsed,
- Cherry tomatoes: 1 cup (150g, 5.29 oz),
- Halved red onion: 1/2, thinly sliced (50g, 1.76 oz),
- Olive oil: 2 tbsp (30ml, 1.01 oz),
- Lemon juice: 1 tbsp (15ml, 0.51 oz),
- Fresh parsley: 2 tbsp, chopped (10g, 0.35 oz),
- Salt and pepper: to taste

Instructions

- **Preparation:** Drain and rinse the tuna and beans. Halve the cherry tomatoes. Thinly slice the red onion. Chop the parsley.
- **Assembly:** In a large bowl, combine the tuna, beans, cherry tomatoes, red onion, and parsley.
- **Dressing:** Drizzle with olive oil and lemon juice. Season with salt and pepper. Toss to combine.
- **Serving:** Serve immediately or chill for 30 minutes to allow flavors to meld.

 Chef's Tips: "Add some capers or olives for extra flavor and brininess."

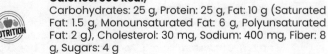 **Calories: 300 kcal,**
Carbohydrates: 25 g, Protein: 25 g, Fat: 10 g (Saturated Fat: 1.5 g, Monounsaturated Fat: 6 g, Polyunsaturated Fat: 2 g), Cholesterol: 30 mg, Sodium: 400 mg, Fiber: 8 g, Sugars: 4 g

 Interesting Fact: Tuna and bean salad is a nutritious and quick Mediterranean dish, popular for its protein and fiber content, making it a healthy meal option.

Stewed Vegetables with Chicken

Country of Origin:
Mediterranean Region

 Prep: 15 mins |  **Cook:** 30 mins | **Total:** 45 mins | **Level:** 2/5 | **Servings:** 2

Ingredients

- Chicken breast: 2 (300g, 10.58 oz),
- Olive oil: 2 tbsp (30ml, 1.01 oz),
- Onion: 1, chopped (150g, 5.29 oz),
- Red bell pepper: 1, chopped (120g, 4.23 oz),
- Zucchini: 1, sliced (150g, 5.29 oz),
- Carrots: 2, sliced (140g, 4.94 oz),
- Canned tomatoes: 1 cup (240g, 8.47 oz),
- Garlic: 2 cloves, minced (6g, 0.21 oz),
- Fresh herbs (e.g., thyme, rosemary): 2 tbsp (10g, 0.35 oz),
- Salt and pepper: to taste

 Calories: Calories: 350 kcal,
Carbohydrates: 20 g, Protein: 35 g, Fat: 15 g (Saturated Fat: 2.5 g, Monounsaturated Fat: 9g, Polyunsaturated Fat: 1.5g), Cholesterol: 90mg, Sodium: 400mg, Fiber: 5g, Sugars: 10 g

 Interesting Fact: Stewed vegetables with chicken is a versatile dish enjoyed across the Mediterranean, reflecting the region's emphasis on fresh, seasonal produce and simple cooking methods.

 Chef's Tips: "For a richer flavor, add a splash of white wine while simmering the vegetables."

Instructions

- **Preparation:** Chop the onion, bell pepper, zucchini, and carrots. Mince the garlic. Cut chicken into bite-sized pieces.
- **Cooking:** Heat olive oil in a large pot over medium heat. Add chicken and cook until browned, about 5 min. Remove chicken and set aside. In the same pot, sauté onion, bell pepper, zucchini, carrots, and garlic for 5 min. Add canned tomatoes and herbs, season with salt and pepper. Return chicken to the pot, cover, and simmer for 20 min. Stir occasionally to ensure even cooking.
- **Serving:** Serve hot, garnished with fresh herbs.

Garlic Shrimp with Parsley

Country of Origin:
Spain

 Prep: 10 mins | **Cook:** 10 mins | **Total:** 20 mins | **Level:** 1/5 | **Servings:** 2

Ingredients

- Shrimp: 300g (10.58 oz), peeled and deveined,
- Olive oil: 2 tbsp (30ml, 1.01 oz),
- Garlic: 4 cloves, minced (12g, 0.42 oz),
- Fresh parsley: 2 tbsp, chopped (10g, 0.35 oz),
- Lemon juice: 1 tbsp (15ml, 0.51 oz),
- Salt and pepper: to taste,
- Red pepper flakes: 1/2 tsp (1g, 0.03 oz)

Instructions

- **Preparation:** Mince the garlic and chop the parsley. Season shrimp with salt and pepper.
- **Cooking:** Heat olive oil in a skillet over medium heat. Add garlic and red pepper flakes, sauté for 1 min. Add shrimp, cook for 2-3 min per side until pink and opaque.
- **Assembly:** Remove skillet from heat, stir in lemon juice and parsley.
- **Serving:** Serve hot, garnished with extra parsley. Pair with crusty bread or a fresh salad.

 Chef's Tips: "For added flavor, marinate shrimp in olive oil, garlic, and lemon juice for 30 minI before cooking."

Calories: 250 kcal,
Carbohydrates: 3 g, Protein: 25 g, Fat: 15 g (Saturated Fat: 2.5 g, Monounsaturated Fat: 10 g, Polyunsaturated Fat: 2.5g), Cholesterol: 200mg, Sodium: 600mg, Fiber: 1g, Sugars: 1g

 Interesting Fact: Garlic shrimp, or "gambas al ajillo," is a popular tapa in Spain, celebrated for its bold flavors and simplicity.

31 Chicken and Vegetable Casserole

Country of Origin: Mediterranean Region

 Prep: 20 mins | **Cook:** 40 mins | **Total:** 60 mins | **Level:** 3/5 | **Servings:** 2

Ingredients

- Chicken breast: 2 (300g, 10.58 oz),
- Olive oil: 2 tbsp (30ml, 1.01 oz),
- Onion: 1, chopped (150g, 5.29 oz),
- Red bell pepper: 1, chopped (120g, 4.23 oz),
- Zucchini: 1, sliced (150g, 5.29 oz),
- Carrots: 2, sliced (140g, 4.94 oz),
- Canned tomatoes: 1 cup (240g, 8.47 oz),
- Garlic: 2 cloves, minced (6g, 0.21 oz),
- Fresh herbs (e.g., thyme, rosemary): 2 tbsp (10g, 0.35 oz),
- Cheese (e.g., feta or mozzarella): 1/2 cup, grated (60g, 2.12 oz),
- Salt and pepper: to taste.

Instructions

- **Preparation:** Preheat the oven to 375ºF (190ºC). Chop vegetables and garlic. Cut chicken into bite-sized pieces.
- **Cooking:** Heat oil in a skillet. Brown chicken, about 5 min. Remove chicken, sauté vegetables and garlic in the same skillet for 5 min. Add tomatoes and herbs, season.
- **Assembly:** In a baking dish, layer chicken and vegetable mixture. Top with grated cheese.
- **Serving:** Bake for 25-30 min, until the cheese is melted and bubbly. Serve hot, garnished with herbs.

Calories: 400 kcal,
Carbohydrates: 20 g, Protein: 35 g, Fat: 20 g (Saturated Fat: 5 g, Monounsaturated Fat: 10 g, Polyunsaturated Fat: 3 g), Cholesterol: 100 mg, Sodium: 450 mg, Fiber: 5 g, Sugars: 10 g

Interesting Fact: This casserole is a comforting dish combining fresh vegetables and tender chicken, typical of Mediterranean home cooking.

Chef's Tips: "Add white wine for richer flavor before baking."

32 Whole Grain Pizza

Country of Origin: Italy

 Prep: 15 mins | **Cook:** 15 mins | **Total:** 30 mins | **Level:** 3/5 | **Servings:** 2

Ingredients

- Whole grain pizza dough: 1 (250g, 8.82 oz),
- Olive oil: 2 tbsp (30ml, 1.01 oz),
- Tomato sauce: 1/2 cup (120g, 4.23 oz),
- Mozzarella cheese: 1 cup, shredded (100g, 3.53 oz),
- Cherry tomatoes: 1 cup, halved (150g, 5.29 oz),
- Fresh basil: 1/4 cup (10g, 0.35 oz),
- Salt and pepper: to taste

Instructions

- **Preparation:** Preheat the oven to 450ºF (230ºC). Roll out the pizza dough on a floured surface.
- **Cooking:** Place dough on a baking sheet. Brush with olive oil, spread tomato sauce, sprinkle with cheese, and add cherry tomatoes. Season with salt and pepper. Bake for 12-15 min, until the crust is golden and the cheese is bubbly.
- **Assembly:** Remove pizza from oven, top with fresh basil.
- **Serving:** Slice and serve hot.

Chef's Tips: "Add your favorite vegetables or lean proteins for variety."

Calories: 350 kcal,
Carbohydrates: 40 g, Protein: 15 g, Fat: 15 g (Saturated Fat: 5 g, Monounsaturated Fat: 7 g, Polyunsaturated Fat: 1 g), Cholesterol: 20 mg, Sodium: 600 mg, Fiber: 6 g, Sugars: 6 g

Interesting Fact: Whole grain pizza provides more fiber and nutrients than traditional pizza.

33 Turkey Meatballs with Tomato Sauce

  Country of Origin: Italy

 Prep: 15 mins | **Cook:** 25 mins | **Total:** 40 mins | **Level:** 3/5 | **Servings:** 2

Ingredients

- Ground turkey: 300g (10.58 oz),
- Olive oil: 2 tbsp (30ml, 1.01 oz),
- Onion: 1, finely chopped (150g, 5.29 oz),
- Garlic: 2 cloves, minced (6g, 0.21 oz),
- Egg: 1 (50g, 1.76 oz),
- Breadcrumbs: 1/4 cup (30g, 1.06 oz),
- Parmesan cheese: 2 tbsp, grated (15g, 0.53 oz),
- Fresh parsley: 2 tbsp, chopped (10g, 0.35 oz),
- Salt and pepper: to taste,
- Canned tomatoes: 1 cup (240g, 8.47 oz),
- Basil: 1 tbsp, chopped (5g, 0.18 oz)

 Calories: 400 kcal,
Carbohydrates: 20 g, Protein: 35 g, Fat: 20 g (Saturated Fat: 5 g, Monounsaturated Fat: 10 g, Polyunsaturated Fat: 3g), Cholesterol: 100mg, Sodium: 450 mg, Fiber: 5g, Sugars: 10 g

 Interesting Fact: Turkey meatballs are a leaner alternative to traditional meatballs, offering the same rich flavors with less fat.

 Chef's Tips: "Serve with whole grain pasta or a side of vegetables for a balanced meal."

Instructions

- **Preparation:** Preheat the oven to 375ºF (190ºC). Mix turkey, egg, breadcrumbs, Parmesan, parsley, salt, and pepper. Form into meatballs.
- **Cooking:** Heat 1 tbsp olive oil in a skillet, brown meatballs on all sides, about 5 min. Transfer to a baking dish. In the same skillet, sauté onion and garlic in remaining olive oil, add tomatoes and basil, season with salt and pepper, and simmer for 10 min.
- **Assembly:** Pour tomato sauce over meatballs.
- **Serving:** Bake for 15 min, until cooked through. Serve hot.

34 Seafood Pasta

 Country of Origin: Italy

 Prep: 10 mins | **Cook:** 15 mins | **Total:** 25 mins | **Level:** 3/5 | **Servings:** 2

Ingredients

- Whole grain pasta: 200g (7.05 oz),
- Mixed seafood (shrimp, mussels, calamari): 300g (10.58 oz),
- Olive oil: 2 tbsp (30ml, 1.01 oz),
- Garlic: 3 cloves, minced (9g, 0.32 oz),
- Cherry tomatoes: 1 cup, halved (150g, 5.29 oz),
- White wine: 1/4 cup (60ml, 2.03 oz),
- Fresh parsley: 2 tbsp, chopped (10g, 0.35 oz),
- Lemon zest: 1 tsp (2g, 0.07 oz),
- Salt and pepper: to taste

Instructions

- **Preparation:** Cook pasta according to package instructions. Mince garlic and halve cherry tomatoes.
- **Cooking:** Heat olive oil in a skillet over medium heat. Sauté garlic for 1 min. Add seafood, cook for 3-5 min. Add cherry tomatoes and white wine, cook for another 5 min. Stir in cooked pasta, parsley, lemon zest, salt, and pepper.
- **Assembly:** Ensure seafood is evenly distributed throughout the pasta.
- **Serving:** Serve hot, garnished with extra parsley.

 Chef's Tips: "Add a pinch of red pepper flakes for a spicy kick."

 Calories: 450 kcal,
Carbohydrates: 50 g, Protein: 30 g, Fat: 15 g (Saturated Fat: 2 g, Monounsaturated Fat: 10 g, Polyunsaturated Fat: 2 g), Cholesterol: 150 mg, Sodium: 500 mg, Fiber: 6 g, Sugars: 6 g

 Interesting Fact: Seafood pasta combines fresh seafood with pasta, making it a favorite in coastal Italian regions.

35 Stewed Meat with Vegetables

Country of Origin: Mediterranean Region

Prep: 15 mins | **Cook:** 60 mins | **Total:** 75 mins | **Level:** 3/5 | **Servings:** 2

Ingredients

- Chicken breast: 2 (300g, 10.58 oz),
- Olive oil: 2 tbsp (30ml, 1.01 oz),
- Onion: 1, chopped (150g, 5.29 oz),
- Red bell pepper: 1, chopped (120g, 4.23 oz),
- Zucchini: 1, sliced (150g, 5.29 oz),
- Carrots: 2, sliced (140g, 4.94 oz),
- Canned tomatoes: 1 cup (240g, 8.47 oz),
- Garlic: 2 cloves, minced (6g, 0.21 oz),
- Fresh herbs (e.g., thyme, rosemary): 2 tbsp (10g, 0.35 oz),
- Cheese (e.g., feta or mozzarella): 1/2 cup, grated (60g, 2.12 oz),
- Salt and pepper: to taste.

Instructions

- **Preparation:** Chop onion, carrots, celery, potatoes, and garlic. Cut beef into bite-sized pieces.
- **Cooking:** Heat olive oil in a large pot. Brown beef, about 5 min. Remove beef, sauté onion, carrots, celery, and garlic in the same pot for 5 min. Add tomatoes, broth, thyme, and beef. Bring to a boil, reduce heat, cover, and simmer for 60 min, adding potatoes halfway through.
- **Assembly:** Stir occasionally to ensure even cooking.
- **Serving:** Serve hot, garnished with fresh thyme.

Calories: 450 kcal,
Carbohydrates: 30 g, Protein: 35 g, Fat: 20 g (Saturated Fat: 5 g, Monounsaturated Fat: 10 g, Polyunsaturated Fat: 2 g), Cholesterol: 100 mg, Sodium: 600 mg, Fiber: 6 g, Sugars: 6 g

Interesting Fact: This hearty dish highlights the Mediterranean focus on wholesome, flavorful ingredients.

Chef's Tips: "For extra flavor, add a splash of red wine while simmering."

36 Vegetable and Cheese Lasagna

Country of Origin: Italy

Prep: 20 mins | **Cook:** 45 mins | **Total:** 65 mins | **Level:** 3/5 | **Servings:** 2

Ingredients

- Lasagna noodles: 6 (150g, 5.29 oz),
- Olive oil: 2 tbsp (30ml, 1.01 oz),
- Zucchini: 1, sliced (150g, 5.29 oz),
- Eggplant: 1, sliced (150g, 5.29 oz),
- Spinach: 2 cups (60g, 2.12 oz),
- Ricotta cheese: 1 cup (240g, 8.47 oz),
- Mozzarella cheese: 1 cup, shredded (100g, 3.53 oz),
- Parmesan cheese: 1/4 cup, grated (30g, 1.06 oz),
- Tomato sauce: 1 cup (240g, 8.47 oz),
- Fresh basil: 1/4 cup, chopped (10g, 0.35 oz),
- Salt and pepper: to taste

Instructions

- **Preparation:** Preheat the oven to 375°F (190°C). Cook lasagna noodles according to package instructions. Slice zucchini and eggplant, chop spinach and basil.
- **Cooking:** Heat olive oil in a skillet, sauté zucchini and eggplant for 5 min. Mix ricotta cheese, spinach, salt, and pepper in a bowl.
- **Assembly:** In a baking dish, layer tomato sauce, lasagna noodles, ricotta mixture, sautéed vegetables, and mozzarella cheese. Repeat layers, top with Parmesan cheese.

- **Serving:** Bake for 35-40 min, until the cheese is bubbly and golden. Serve hot.

Chef's Tips: "Let lasagna rest for 10 minutes before serving for easier slicing."

Calories: 450 kcal,
Carbohydrates: 45g, Protein: 25g, Fat: 20g (Saturated Fat: 10g, Monounsaturated Fat: 6g, Polyunsaturated Fat: 2g), Cholesterol: 60mg, Sodium: 600mg, Fiber: 6g, Sugars: 10g

Interesting Fact: Vegetable and cheese lasagna is a popular Italian dish that showcases layers of fresh vegetables and creamy cheese, providing a hearty and nutritious meal.

37 Fish Cakes with Vegetables

Country of Origin: Mediterranean Region

Prep: 15 mins | **Cook:** 20 mins | **Total:** 35 mins | **Level:** 3/5 | **Servings:** 2

Ingredients

- White fish fillets: 300g (10.58 oz),
- Olive oil: 2 tbsp (30ml, 1.01 oz),
- Potato: 1 large, boiled and mashed (200g, 7.05 oz),
- Carrot: 1, grated (70g, 2.47 oz),
- Onion: 1/2, finely chopped (75g, 2.65 oz),
- Egg: 1 (50g, 1.76 oz),
- Fresh parsley: 2 tbsp, chopped (10g, 0.35 oz),
- Lemon zest: 1 tsp (2g, 0.07 oz),
- Salt and pepper: to taste,
- Breadcrumbs: 1/2 cup (60g, 2.12 oz)

 Calories: 350 kcal,
Carbohydrates: 30 g, Protein: 25 g, Fat: 15 g (Saturated Fat: 2.5 g, Monounsaturated Fat: 8 g, Polyunsaturated Fat: 2 g), Cholesterol: 110 mg, Sodium: 450 mg, Fiber: 5 g, Sugars: 3 g

 Interesting Fact: Fish cakes are a popular dish throughout the Mediterranean, known for their versatility and the ability to incorporate a variety of fresh vegetables and herbs.

 Chef's Tips: "Add a bit of Dijon mustard to the mixture for extra flavor."

Instructions

- **Preparation:** Boil and mash the potato. Grate the carrot, chop the onion and parsley.
- **Cooking:** Cook fish fillets in boiling water until flaky, about 5 min. Flake fish into a bowl, add mashed potato, carrot, onion, egg, parsley, lemon zest, salt, and pepper. Mix well. Shape mixture into patties, coat with breadcrumbs. Heat olive oil in a skillet over medium heat, fry patties for 3-4 min per side until golden.
- **Assembly:** Ensure patties are evenly cooked.
- **Serving:** Serve hot with a side of salad or steamed vegetables.

38 Chicken Spinach Cheese Rolls

Country of Origin: Mediterranean Region

Prep: 15 mins | **Cook:** 25 mins | **Total:** 40 mins | **Level:** 3/5 | **Servings:** 2

Ingredients

- Chicken breasts: 2 (300g, 10.58 oz),
- Fresh spinach: 2 cups (60g, 2.12 oz),
- Feta cheese: 1/2 cup, crumbled (60g, 2.12 oz),
- Olive oil: 2 tbsp (30ml, 1.01 oz),
- Garlic: 2 cloves, minced (6g, 0.21 oz),
- Lemon juice: 1 tbsp (15ml, 0.51 oz),
- Salt and pepper: to taste,
- Toothpicks or kitchen twine

Instructions

- **Preparation:** Preheat the oven to 375ºF (190ºC). Pound chicken breasts to even thickness. Sauté spinach and garlic in olive oil until wilted, about 3 min. Mix spinach with feta cheese, lemon juice, salt, and pepper.
- **Assembly:** Place spinach mixture on each chicken breast, roll up tightly, and secure with toothpicks or twine.
- **Cooking:** Heat olive oil in a skillet over medium heat, sear chicken rolls until browned, about 3 min per side. Transfer to a baking dish and bake for 15 min, until cooked through.
- **Serving:** Slice and serve hot.

 Chef's Tips: "Add sun-dried tomatoes to the filling for extra flavor."

 Calories: 350 kcal,
Carbohydrates: 4 g, Protein: 35 g, Fat: 20 g (Saturated Fat: 5 g, Monounsaturated Fat: 10 g, Polyunsaturated Fat: 2 g), Cholesterol: 100 mg, Sodium: 450 mg, Fiber: 1 g, Sugars: 1 g

 Interesting Fact: Chicken rolls are popular for their versatility, allowing various fillings and seasonings, and are a staple in Mediterranean cuisine.

39 Roasted Potatoes with Herbs

 **Country of Origin:** Mediterranean Region

Prep: 10 mins | **Cook:** 40 mins | **Total:** 50 mins | **Level:** 2/5 | **Servings:** 2

Ingredients

- Potatoes: 4 medium, diced (600g, 21.16 oz),
- Olive oil: 2 tbsp (30ml, 1.01 oz),
- Fresh rosemary: 1 tbsp, chopped (5g, 0.18 oz),
- Fresh thyme: 1 tbsp, chopped (5g, 0.18 oz),
- Garlic: 3 cloves, minced (9g, 0.32 oz),
- Salt and pepper: to taste

Instructions

- **Preparation:** Preheat the oven to 400ºF (200ºC). Dice potatoes into evenly sized pieces. Mince garlic and chop herbs.
- **Cooking:** Toss potatoes with olive oil, garlic, rosemary, thyme, salt, and pepper. Spread on a baking sheet in a single layer. Roast for 35-40 min, turning occasionally, until golden and crispy.
- **Assembly:** Ensure potatoes are evenly coated with herbs and oil.
- **Serving:** Serve hot, garnished with extra fresh herbs if desired.

 Calories: 250 kcal,
Carbohydrates: 45 g, Protein: 5 g, Fat: 8 g (Saturated Fat: 1 g, Monounsaturated Fat: 5 g, Polyunsaturated Fat: 1 g), Cholesterol: 0 mg, Sodium: 300 mg, Fiber: 5 g, Sugars: 2g

 Interesting Fact: Roasted potatoes with herbs are a classic Mediterranean side dish, highlighting the use of fresh, aromatic herbs.

 Chef's Tips: "Add a squeeze of lemon juice before serving for a fresh twist."

40 Minestrone Soup

 **Country of Origin:** Italy

Prep: 15 mins | **Cook:** 45 mins | **Total:** 60 mins | **Level:** 3/5 | **Servings:** 2

Ingredients

- Olive oil: 2 tbsp (30ml, 1.01 oz),
- Onion: 1, chopped (150g, 5.29 oz),
- Carrot: 1, chopped (70g, 2.47 oz),
- Celery: 2 stalks, chopped (100g, 3.53 oz),
- Zucchini: 1, diced (150g, 5.29 oz),
- Canned tomatoes: 1 cup (240g, 8.47 oz),
- Vegetable broth: 4 cups (960ml, 32.47 oz),
- Kidney beans: 1 can (240g, 8.47 oz),
- Pasta: 1/2 cup (50g, 1.76 oz),
- Fresh basil: 1/4 cup, chopped (10g, 0.35 oz),
- Salt and pepper: to taste

Instructions

- **Preparation:** Chop the onion, carrot, celery, and zucchini. Rinse and drain the beans.
- **Cooking:** Heat olive oil in a large pot over medium heat. Sauté onion, carrot, and celery for 5 min. Add zucchini and cook for another 3 min. Stir in canned tomatoes and vegetable broth, bring to a boil. Reduce heat and simmer for 20 min. Add beans and pasta, cook until pasta is al dente, about 10 min.
- **Assembly:** Stir in fresh basil, season with salt and pepper.
- **Serving:** Serve hot, garnished with extra basil if desired.

 Chef's Tips: "For added flavor, sprinkle some grated Parmesan cheese on top before serving"

 Calories: 300 kcal,
Carbohydrates: 45 g, Protein: 10 g, Fat: 10 g (Saturated Fat: 1.5 g, Monounsaturated Fat: 6 g, Polyunsaturated Fat: 1 g), Cholesterol: 0 mg, Sodium: 800 mg, Fiber: 8 g, Sugars: 10 g

 Interesting Fact: Minestrone soup is a traditional Italian soup made with seasonal vegetables and often includes pasta or rice.

41 Grilled Fish with Vegetables

Country of Origin: Mediterranean Region

Prep: 10 mins | **Cook:** 15 mins | **Total:** 25 mins | **Level:** 2/5 | **Servings:** 2

Ingredients

- White fish fillets: 2 (300g, 10.58 oz),
- Olive oil: 2 tbsp (30ml, 1.01 oz),
- Zucchini: 1, sliced (150g, 5.29 oz),
- Red or Yellow Bell pepper: 1, sliced (120g, 4.23 oz),
- Cherry tomatoes: 1 cup (150g, 5.29 oz),
- Lemon: 1, sliced (100g, 3.53 oz),
- Fresh herbs (e.g., parsley, thyme): 2 tbsp, chopped (10g, 0.35 oz),
- Garlic: 2 cloves, Salt and pepper: to taste

 Calories: 350 kcal,
Carbohydrates: 10 g, Protein: 35 g, Fat: 18 g (Saturated Fat: 3 g, Monounsaturated Fat: 10 g, Polyunsaturated Fat: 2 g), Cholesterol: 70 mg, Sodium: 300 mg, Fiber: 3 g, Sugars: 6g

 Interesting Fact: Grilled fish with vegetables is a staple in Mediterranean cuisine, known for its simplicity and health benefits.

 Chef's Tips: "Marinate the fish in lemon juice and herbs for 15 minutes before grilling for extra flavor."

Instructions

- **Preparation:** Preheat grill to medium-high heat. Slice vegetables and lemon. Mince garlic and chop herbs.
- **Cooking:** Brush fish and vegetables with olive oil, season with garlic, herbs, salt, and pepper. Grill fish for 3-4 min per side until cooked through. Grill vegetables for 8-10 min, turning occasionally.
- **Assembly:** Arrange grilled fish and vegetables on a serving platter.
- **Serving:** Garnish with lemon slices and fresh herbs. Serve hot.

42 Bean and Corn Salad

Country of Origin: Mediterranean Region

Prep: 10 mins | **Cook:** 0 mins | **Total:** 10 mins | **Level:** 1/5 | **Servings:** 2

Ingredients

- Canned black beans: 1 cup (240g, 8.47 oz),
- Corn kernels: 1 cup (150g, 5.29 oz),
- Cherry tomatoes: 1 cup, halved (150g, 5.29 oz),
- Red onion: 1/2, finely chopped (50g, 1.76 oz),
- Fresh cilantro: 1/4 cup, chopped (10g, 0.35 oz),
- Olive oil: 2 tbsp (30ml, 1.01 oz),
- Lime juice: 1 tbsp (15ml, 0.51 oz), Salt and pepper: to taste

Instructions

- **Preparation:** Drain and rinse the beans. Halve the cherry tomatoes and finely chop the red onion and cilantro.
- **Assembly:** In a large bowl, combine black beans, corn, cherry tomatoes, red onion, and cilantro.
- **Dressing:** Drizzle with olive oil and lime juice. Season with salt and pepper. Toss to combine.
- **Serving:** Serve immediately or chill for 30 minutes to allow flavors to meld.

 Chef's Tips: ""Add diced avocado for extra creaminess and nutrition."

 Calories: 250 kcal,
Carbohydrates: 35 g, Protein: 8 g, Fat: 10 g (Saturated Fat: 1.5 g, Monounsaturated Fat: 6 g, Polyunsaturated Fat: 1 g), Cholesterol: 0 mg, Sodium: 300 mg, Fiber: 10 g, Sugars: 6 g

 Interesting Fact: Bean and corn salad is a vibrant and refreshing dish that reflects the Mediterranean diet's emphasis on fresh, plant-based ingredients.

 43 # Chicken Fillet with Broccoli & Lemon

Country of Origin:
Mediterranean Region

 Prep: 10 mins | **Cook:** 20 mins | **Total:** 30 mins | **Level:** 2/5 | **Servings:** 2

Ingredients

- Chicken fillets: 2 (300g, 10.58 oz),
- Olive oil: 2 tbsp (30ml, 1.01 oz),
- Broccoli florets: 2 cups (150g, 5.29 oz),
- Garlic: 2 cloves, minced (6g, 0.21 oz),
- Lemon juice: 2 tbsp (30ml, 1.01 oz),
- Lemon zest: 1 tsp (2g, 0.07 oz),
- Salt and pepper: to taste,
- Fresh parsley: 1 tbsp, chopped (5g, 0.18 oz)

 Calories: 350 kcal,
Carbohydrates: 10 g, Protein: 35 g, Fat: 18 g (Saturated Fat: 3g, Monounsaturated Fat: 10 g, Polyunsaturated Fat: 2 g), Cholesterol: 90 mg, Sodium: 300 mg, Fiber: 4 g, Sugars: 3 g

 Interesting Fact: This dish combines lean protein with nutrient-rich broccoli and zesty lemon, reflecting the Mediterranean diet's focus on fresh, wholesome ingredients.

 Chef's Tips: "Add a sprinkle of red pepper flakes for a hint of heat."

Instructions

- **Preparation:** Preheat the oven to 375°F (190°C). Mince garlic and chop parsley.
- **Cooking:** Heat olive oil in a skillet over medium heat. Season chicken with salt and pepper. Sear chicken fillets for 3-4 min per side until golden brown. Transfer to a baking dish. In the same skillet, add broccoli and garlic, sauté for 2-3 min. Add lemon juice and zest, cook for another 2 min. Pour broccoli mixture over chicken fillets.
- **Assembly:** Bake for 15 min, until chicken is cooked through and broccoli is tender.
- **Serving:** Serve hot, garnished with fresh parsley.

 **44** # Lentil Stew with Vegetables

Country of Origin:
Mediterranean Region

 Prep: 10 mins | **Cook:** 40 mins | **Total:** 50 mins | **Level:** 2/5 | **Servings:** 2

Ingredients

- Green or brown lentils: 1 cup (200g, 7.05 oz),
- Olive oil: 2 tbsp (30ml, 1.01 oz),
- Onion: 1, chopped (150g, 5.29 oz),
- Carrots: 2, chopped (140g, 4.94 oz),
- Celery: 2 stalks, chopped (100g, 3.53 oz),
- Garlic: 2 cloves, minced (6g, 0.21 oz),
- Canned tomatoes: 1 cup (240g, 8.47 oz),
- Vegetable broth: 4 cups (960ml, 32.47 oz),
- Bay leaf: 1,
- Fresh thyme: 1 tsp (1g, 0.04 oz),
- Salt and pepper: to taste

 Chef's Tips: "Add a splash of red wine for a richer flavor."

 Calories: 350 kcal,
Carbohydrates: 50 g, Protein: 15 g, Fat: 10 g (Saturated Fat: 1.5 g, Monounsaturated Fat: 6 g, Polyunsaturated Fat: 1 g), Cholesterol: 0 mg, Sodium: 600 mg, Fiber: 15 g, Sugars: 10 g

 Interesting Fact: Lentil stew is a staple in Mediterranean diets, offering a hearty and nutritious meal that's high in fiber and protein.

Instructions

- **Preparation:** Rinse lentils and chop onion, carrots, and celery. Mince garlic.
- **Cooking:** Heat olive oil in a large pot over medium heat. Sauté onion, carrots, celery, and garlic for 5 min. Add lentils, tomatoes, broth, bay leaf, thyme, salt, and pepper. Bring to a boil, reduce heat, and simmer for 35 min, until lentils are tender.
- **Assembly:** Remove bay leaf.
- **Serving:** Serve hot, garnished with fresh thyme.

Quinoa with Vegetables & Greens

Country of Origin:
Mediterranean Region

Prep: 10 mins | **Cook:** 20 mins | **Total:** 30 mins | **Level:** 2/5 | **Servings:** 2

Ingredients

- Quinoa: 1 cup (185g, 6.53 oz),
- Olive oil: 2 tbsp (30ml, 1.01 oz),
- Onion: 1, chopped (150g, 5.29 oz),
- Red or yellow Bell pepper: 1, chopped (120g, 4.23 oz),
- Zucchini: 1, diced (150g, 5.29 oz),
- Spinach: 2 cups (60g, 2.12 oz),
- Garlic: 2 cloves, minced (6g, 0.21 oz),
- Vegetable broth: 2 cups (480ml, 16.91 oz),
- Lemon juice: 1 tbsp (15ml, 0.51 oz),
- Fresh parsley: 1/4 cup, chopped (10g, 0.35 oz),
- Salt and pepper: to taste.

 Calories: 300 kcal,
Carbohydrates: 50 g, Protein: 10 g, Fat: 10 g (Saturated Fat: 1.5 g, Monounsaturated Fat: 6 g, Polyunsaturated Fat: 1 g), Cholesterol: 0 mg, Sodium: 500 mg, Fiber: 8 g, Sugars: 6 g

 Interesting Fact: Quinoa is a versatile grain that has been cultivated for thousands of years, known for its high protein content and nutritious benefits.

 Chef's Tips: "Add roasted nuts or seeds for extra crunch and protein."

Instructions

- **Preparation:** Rinse quinoa under cold water. Chop onion, bell pepper, zucchini, and garlic.
- **Cooking:** Heat olive oil in a pot over medium heat. Sauté onion, bell pepper, zucchini, and garlic for 5 min. Add quinoa and vegetable broth. Bring to a boil, reduce heat, cover, and simmer for 15 min until quinoa is cooked. Stir in spinach until wilted. Add lemon juice, parsley, salt, and pepper.
- **Assembly:** Fluff quinoa with a fork.
- **Serving:** Serve hot, garnished with extra parsley.

Tomato Basil Soup

Country of Origin:
Italy

Prep: 10 mins | **Cook:** 30 mins | **Total:** 40 mins | **Level:** 2/5 | **Servings:** 2

Ingredients

- Olive oil: 2 tbsp (30ml, 1.01 oz),
- Onion: 1, chopped (150g, 5.29 oz),
- Garlic: 2 cloves, minced (6g, 0.21 oz),
- Canned tomatoes: 2 cups (480g, 16.91 oz),
- Vegetable broth: 2 cups (480ml, 16.91 oz),
- Fresh basil: 1/4 cup, chopped (10g, 0.35 oz),
- Salt and pepper: to taste,
- Heavy cream: 1/4 cup (60ml, 2.03 oz) (optional)

Instructions

- **Preparation:** Chop onion and garlic.
- **Cooking:** Heat olive oil in a pot over medium heat. Sauté onion and garlic for 5 min. Add canned tomatoes and vegetable broth. Bring to a boil, reduce heat, and simmer for 20 min. Stir in basil, salt, and pepper. For a creamy texture, add heavy cream and simmer for another 5 min.
- **Assembly:** Blend the soup until smooth using an immersion blender or in batches in a blender.
- **Serving:** Serve hot, garnished with fresh basil leaves.

 Chef's Tips: "Add a pinch of red pepper flakes for a spicy kick."

 Calories: 200 kcal,
Carbohydrates: 25 g, Protein: 4 g, Fat: 10 g (Saturated Fat: 3 g, Monounsaturated Fat: 5 g, Polyunsaturated Fat: 1 g), Cholesterol: 15 mg, Sodium: 700 mg, Fiber: 4 g, Sugars: 12 g

 Interesting Fact: Tomato basil soup is a classic Italian dish known for its rich flavor and simplicity, often enjoyed with a side of crusty bread.

Instructions

- **Preparation:** Rinse buckwheat. Chop onion, garlic, bell pepper, zucchini, and slice mushrooms.
- **Cooking:** Heat olive oil in a pot over medium heat. Sauté onion and garlic for 5 min. Add mushrooms, bell pepper, and zucchini, cook for another 5 min. Stir in buckwheat and vegetable broth. Bring to a boil, reduce heat, cover, and simmer for 15 min until buckwheat is tender.
- **Assembly:** Fluff buckwheat with a fork, mix in fresh parsley, season with salt and pepper.
- **Serving:** Serve hot, garnished with extra parsley if desired.

 Chef's Tips: "Add a sprinkle of feta cheese for extra flavor."

 Calories: 250 kcal,
Carbohydrates: 8 g, Protein: 20 g, Fat: 16 g (Saturated Fat: 2.5 g, Monounsaturated Fat: 10 g, Polyunsaturated Fat: 2 g), Cholesterol: 30 mg, Sodium: 400 mg, Fiber: 2 g, Sugars: 4 g

 Interesting Fact: This tuna salad is a staple in Mediterranean diets, highlighting fresh and flavorful ingredients that are rich in healthy fats and protein.

 # Buckwheat with Mushrooms and Vegetables

Country of Origin: Mediterranean Region

 Prep: 10 mins | **Cook:** 20 mins | **Total:** 30 mins | **Level:** 2/5 | **Servings:** 2

Ingredients

- Buckwheat: 1 cup (180g, 6.35 oz),
- Olive oil: 2 tbsp (30ml, 1.01 oz),
- Onion: 1, chopped (150g, 5.29 oz),
- Garlic: 2 cloves, minced (6g, 0.21 oz),
- Mushrooms: 1 cup, sliced (150g, 5.29 oz),
- Red Bell pepper: 1, chopped (120g, 4.23 oz),
- Zucchini: 1, diced (150g, 5.29 oz),
- Vegetable broth: 2 cups (480ml, 16.91 oz),
- Fresh parsley: 1/4 cup, chopped (10g, 0.35 oz),
- Salt and pepper: to taste

 Calories: 350 kcal,
Carbohydrates: 55 g, Protein: 10 g, Fat: 10 g (Saturated Fat: 1.5 g, Monounsaturated Fat: 6 g, Polyunsaturated Fat: 1 g), Cholesterol: 0 mg, Sodium: 500 mg, Fiber: 8 g, Sugars: 6 g

 Interesting Fact: Buckwheat is gluten-free and rich in protein and fiber

 Chef's Tips: "Add a splash of soy sauce for extra depth of flavor."

 # Tuna with Tomatoes & Olives

 Country of Origin: Mediterranean Region

 Prep: 10 mins | **Cook:** 10 mins | **Total:** 20 mins | **Level:** 2/5 | **Servings:** 2

Ingredients

- Canned tuna: 1 can (150g, 5.29 oz),
- Cherry tomatoes: 1 cup, halved (150g, 5.29 oz),
- Black olives: 1/2 cup, sliced (75g, 2.65 oz),
- Red onion: 1/2, thinly sliced (50g, 1.76 oz),
- Olive oil: 2 tbsp (30ml, 1.01 oz),
- Fresh basil: 1/4 cup, chopped (10g, 0.35 oz),
- Lemon juice: 1 tbsp (15ml, 0.51 oz),
- Salt and pepper: to taste

Instructions

- **Preparation:** Halve cherry tomatoes, slice black olives and red onion, chop fresh basil.
- **Assembly:** In a large bowl, combine tuna, cherry tomatoes, black olives, red onion, and basil. Drizzle with olive oil and lemon juice. Season with salt and pepper.
- **Serving:** Serve immediately or chill for 15 minutes to allow flavors to meld.

49 Baked Sea Bass with Herbs

Country of Origin:
Mediterranean Region

 Prep: 10 mins | **Cook:** 20 mins | **Total:** 30 mins | **Level:** 2/5 | **Servings:** 2

Ingredients

- Sea bass: 2 small (600g, 21.16 oz),
- Olive oil: 2 tbsp (30ml, 1.01 oz),
- Fresh parsley: 1/4 cup, chopped (10g, 0.35 oz),
- Fresh dill: 1/4 cup, chopped (10g, 0.35 oz),
- Garlic: 2 cloves, minced (6g, 0.21 oz),
- Lemon: 1, sliced (100g, 3.53 oz),
- Salt and pepper: to taste

 Calories: 350 kcal,
Carbohydrates: 2 g, Protein: 35 g, Fat: 20 g (Saturated Fat: 3 g, Monounsaturated Fat: 14 g, Polyunsaturated Fat: 3 g), Cholesterol: 85 mg, Sodium: 200 mg, Fiber: 1 g, Sugars: 1 g

 Interesting Fact: Sea bass, known for its delicate flavor and tender texture, is a popular fish in Mediterranean cuisine. It is often prepared with simple, fresh ingredients to highlight its natural taste.

 Chef's Tips: "For a burst of flavor, add a splash of white wine or a sprinkle of capers before baking. Pair with a side of roasted vegetables or a fresh green salad."

Instructions

- **Preparation:** Preheat the oven to 375°F (190°C). Chop parsley and dill, mince garlic, slice lemon.
- **Cooking:** Place Sea bass on a baking sheet lined with parchment paper. Drizzle with olive oil, top with parsley, dill, and garlic. Season with salt and pepper. Arrange lemon slices on top. Bake for 20 min until Sea bass is cooked through and flakes easily with a fork.
- **Assembly:** Ensure herbs and lemon slices are evenly distributed.
- **Serving:** Serve hot, garnished with additional fresh herbs if desired.

50 Rosemary Lemon Chicken

Country of Origin:
Mediterranean Region

 Prep: 10 mins |  **Cook:** 25 mins | **Total:** 35 mins | **Level:** 2/5 | **Servings:** 2

Ingredients

- Olive oil: 2 tbsp (30ml, 1.01 oz),
- Onion: 1, chopped (150g, 5.29 oz),
- Garlic: 2 cloves, minced (6g, 0.21 oz),
- Canned tomatoes: 2 cups (480g, 16.91 oz),
- Vegetable broth: 2 cups (480ml, 16.91 oz),
- Fresh basil: 1/4 cup, chopped (10g, 0.35 oz),
- Salt and pepper: to taste,
- Heavy cream: 1/4 cup (60ml, 2.03 oz) (optional)

Instructions

- **Preparation:** Chop onion and garlic.
- **Cooking:** Heat olive oil in a pot over medium heat. Sauté onion and garlic for 5 min. Add canned tomatoes and vegetable broth. Bring to a boil, reduce heat, and simmer for 20 min. Stir in basil, salt, and pepper. For a creamy texture, add heavy cream and simmer for another 5 min.
- **Assembly:** Blend the soup until smooth using an immersion blender or in batches in a blender.
- **Serving:** Serve hot, garnished with fresh basil leaves.

 Chef's Tips: "Pair with a side of roasted potatoes or steamed vegetables."

 Calories: 320 kcal,
Carbohydrates: 3 g, Protein: 30 g, Fat: 20 g (Saturated Fat: 3 g, Monounsaturated Fat: 12 g, Polyunsaturated Fat: 2 g), Cholesterol: 70 mg, Sodium: 300 mg, Fiber: 1 g, Sugars: 1 g

 Interesting Fact: This dish combines aromatic rosemary and lemon, highlighting the simplicity and flavor typical of Mediterranean cuisine.

END YOUR DAY DELICIOUSLY

SATISFYING MEDITERRANEAN DINNER RECIPES

Ingredients

- White fish fillets: 2 (300g, 10.58 oz),
- Olive oil: 2 tbsp (30ml, 1.01 oz),
- Onion: 1, chopped (150g, 5.29 oz),
- Bell pepper: 1, chopped (120g, 4.23 oz),
- Zucchini: 1, sliced (150g, 5.29 oz),
- Tomato: 2, chopped (300g, 10.58 oz),
- Garlic: 2 cloves, minced (6g, 0.21 oz),
- Vegetable broth: 1 cup (240ml, 8.12 oz),
- Fresh parsley: 1/4 cup, chopped (10g, 0.35 oz),
- Lemon juice: 1 tbsp (15ml, 0.51 oz),
- Salt and pepper: to taste

51 Stewed Vegetables with Fish

Country of Origin: Mediterranean Region

Prep: 15 mins | **Cook:** 30 mins | **Total:** 45 mins | **Level:** 2/5 | **Servings:** 2

Instructions

- **Preparation:** Chop the onion, bell pepper, zucchini, tomatoes, and garlic.
- **Cooking:** Heat olive oil in a large pot over medium heat. Sauté onion and garlic for 5 min. Add bell pepper and zucchini, cook for another 5 min. Stir in tomatoes and vegetable broth, bring to a simmer. Add fish fillets on top, cover, and cook for 15 min until fish is cooked through and vegetables are tender.
- **Assembly:** Remove from heat, stir in lemon juice, and season with salt and pepper.
- **Serving:** Serve hot, garnished with fresh parsley.

 Interesting Fact: This dish showcases the Mediterranean diet's emphasis on fresh vegetables and lean proteins, offering a nutritious and flavorful meal.

 Calories: 300 kcal,
Carbohydrates: 15 g, Protein: 25 g, Fat: 15 g (Saturated Fat: 2.5 g, Monounsaturated Fat: 8 g, Polyunsaturated Fat: 2 g), Cholesterol: 70 mg, Sodium: 400 mg, Fiber: 4 g, Sugars: 8 g

 Chef's Tips: "Add a pinch of red pepper flakes for a bit of heat."

52 Vegetable Broth Soup

Country of Origin:
 Mediterranean Region

 Prep: 10 mins | Cook: 30 mins | Total: 40 mins | Level: 1/5 | Servings: 2

Ingredients

- Olive oil: 2 tbsp (30ml, 1.01 oz),
- Onion: 1, chopped (150g, 5.29 oz),
- Carrots: 2, chopped (140g, 4.94 oz),
- Celery: 2 stalks, chopped (100g, 3.53 oz),
- Garlic: 2 cloves, minced (6g, 0.21 oz),
- Zucchini: 1, sliced (150g, 5.29 oz),
- Tomatoes: 2, chopped (300g, 10.58 oz),
- Vegetable broth: 4 cups (960ml, 32.47 oz),
- Fresh parsley: 1/4 cup, chopped (10g, 0.35 oz),
- Salt and pepper: to taste

 Calories: 150 kcal,
Carbohydrates: 25 g, Protein: 3 g, Fat: 6 g (Saturated Fat: 1 g, Monounsaturated Fat: 3 g, Polyunsaturated Fat: 1 g), Cholesterol: 0 mg, Sodium: 600 mg, Fiber: 5 g, Sugars: 10 g

 Interesting Fact: Vegetable broth soup is a staple in Mediterranean diets, providing a light yet nutritious meal that can be easily customized with seasonal vegetables.

 Chef's Tips: "Add a bay leaf during cooking for additional flavor, and remove it before serving."

Instructions

- **Preparation:** Chop the onion, carrots, celery, zucchini, and tomatoes. Mince the garlic.
- **Cooking:** Heat olive oil in a large pot over medium heat. Sauté onion, carrots, celery, and garlic for 5 min. Add zucchini and tomatoes, cook for another 5 min. Pour in vegetable broth, bring to a boil. Reduce heat, cover, and simmer for 20 min until vegetables are tender.
- **Assembly:** Stir in fresh parsley, season with salt and pepper.
- **Serving:** Serve hot, garnished with extra parsley if desired.

53 Baked Chicken with Potatoes and Herbs

Country of Origin:
 Mediterranean Region

 Prep: 10 mins | Cook: 45 mins | Total: 55 mins |  Level: 2/5 | Servings: 2

Ingredients

- Chicken thighs: 4 (500g, 17.64 oz),
- Potatoes: 4 medium, chopped (600g, 21.16 oz),
- Olive oil: 3 tbsp (45ml, 1.52 oz),
- Fresh rosemary: 2 tbsp, chopped (10g, 0.35 oz),
- Fresh thyme: 2 tbsp, chopped (10g, 0.35 oz),
- Garlic: 4 cloves, minced (12g, 0.42 oz),
- Lemon juice: 2 tbsp (30ml, 1.01 oz),
- Salt and pepper: to taste

Instructions

- **Preparation:** Preheat the oven to 400ºF (200ºC). Chop potatoes and mince garlic.
- **Cooking:** In a large bowl, toss chicken thighs and potatoes with olive oil, rosemary, thyme, garlic, lemon juice, salt, and pepper. Transfer to a baking dish. Bake for 45 min, stirring halfway through, until chicken is cooked and potatoes are golden.
- **Assembly:** Ensure herbs and garlic are evenly distributed over chicken and potatoes.
- **Serving:** Serve hot, garnished with fresh herbs.

 Chef's Tips: "For extra crispiness, broil for the last 5 minutes of cooking."

 Calories: 450 kcal,
Carbohydrates: 30 g, Protein: 30 g, Fat: 25 g (Saturated Fat: 6 g, Monounsaturated Fat: 14 g, Polyunsaturated Fat: 2 g), Cholesterol: 100 mg, Sodium: 400 mg, Fiber: 4g, Sugars: 2 g

 Interesting Fact: This dish is a Mediterranean favorite, combining simple ingredients with fresh herbs for a hearty, flavorful meal.

Instructions

- **Preparation:** Chop onion, carrots, celery, zucchini, and minced garlic.
- **Cooking:** Heat olive oil in a large pot over medium heat. Sauté onion, carrots, and celery for 5 min. Add zucchini and garlic, cook for another 3 min. Stir in chickpeas, tomatoes, vegetable broth, cumin, and paprika. Bring to a boil, reduce heat, and simmer for 20 min until vegetables are tender.
- **Assembly:** Stir in fresh parsley, season with salt and pepper.
- **Serving:** Serve hot, garnished with extra parsley if desired.

 Chef's Tips: "Add a splash of red wine for extra depth of flavor."

 Calories: 400 kcal,
Carbohydrates: 35 g, Protein: 30 g, Fat: 15 g (Saturated Fat: 5 g, Monounsaturated Fat: 8 g, Polyunsaturated Fat: 1 g), Cholesterol: 80 mg, Sodium: 600 mg, Fiber: 6 g, Sugars: 8 g

Interesting Fact: This hearty beef stew highlights the Mediterranean diet's use of fresh vegetables and lean meats for a balanced and flavorful meal.

 # Chickpea and Vegetable Stew

 Country of Origin:
Mediterranean Region

 Prep: 10 mins | **Cook:** 30 mins | **Total:** 40 mins | **Level:** 2/5 | **Servings:** 2

Ingredients

- Canned chickpeas: 1 cup (240g, 8.47 oz),
- Olive oil: 2 tbsp (30ml, 1.01 oz),
- Onion: 1, chopped (150g, 5.29 oz),
- Carrots: 2, chopped (140g, 4.94 oz),
- Celery: 2 stalks, chopped (100g, 3.53 oz),
- Zucchini: 1, diced (150g, 5.29 oz),
- Canned tomatoes: 1 cup (240g, 8.47 oz),
- Vegetable broth: 2 cups (480ml, 16.91 oz),
- Garlic: 2 cloves, minced (6g, 0.21 oz),
- Fresh parsley: 1/4 cup, chopped (10g, 0.35 oz),
- Cumin: 1 tsp (2g, 0.07 oz),
- Paprika: 1 tsp (2g, 0.07 oz),
- Salt and pepper: to taste

 Calories: 300 kcal,
Carbohydrates: 45 g, Protein: 10 g, Fat: 10 g (Saturated Fat: 1.5 g, Monounsaturated Fat: 6 g, Polyunsaturated Fat: 1 g), Cholesterol: 0 mg, Sodium: 600 mg, Fiber: 10 g, Sugars: 10 g

 Interesting Fact: Chickpeas, also known as garbanzo beans, are a staple in Mediterranean diets, valued for their high protein and fiber content.

 Chef's Tips: "Add a squeeze of lemon juice for extra brightness."

 # Beef Stew with Vegetables

 Country of Origin:
Mediterranean Region

 Prep: 15 mins | **Cook:** 1hr 30 mins | **Total:** 1hr 45 mins | **Level:** 3/5 | **Servings:** 2

Ingredients

- Beef stew meat: 300g (10.58 oz),
- Olive oil: 2 tbsp (30ml, 1.01 oz),
- Onion: 1, chopped (150g, 5.29 oz),
- Carrots: 2, chopped (140g, 4.94 oz),
- Celery: 2 stalks, chopped (100g, 3.53 oz),
- Potatoes: 2 medium, diced (300g, 10.58 oz),
- Tomatoes: 2, chopped (300g, 10.58 oz),
- Garlic: 2 cloves, minced (6g, 0.21 oz),
- Beef broth: 2 cups (480ml, 16.91 oz),
- Fresh thyme: 1 tsp (1g, 0.04 oz),
- Bay leaf: 1, Salt and pepper: to taste.

Instructions

- **Preparation:** Chop the onion, carrots, celery, potatoes, and tomatoes. Mince the garlic.
- **Cooking:** Heat olive oil in a large pot over medium heat. Brown the beef for 5 min. Add onion, garlic, carrots, and celery, cook for another 5 min. Add potatoes, tomatoes, beef broth, thyme, and bay leaf. Bring to a boil, reduce heat, cover, and simmer for 1 hr 30 min until beef is tender and vegetables are cooked.
- **Assembly:** Remove bay leaf.
- **Serving:** Serve hot, garnished with fresh thyme.

56 Spaghetti with Garlic and Olive Oil

 Country of Origin: Italy

 Prep: 5 mins | **Cook:** 15 mins | **Total:** 20 mins | **Level:** 1/5 | **Servings:** 2

Ingredients

- Spaghetti: 200g (7.05 oz),
- Olive oil: 1/4 cup (60ml, 2.03 oz),
- Garlic: 4 cloves, thinly sliced (12g, 0.42 oz),
- Red pepper flakes: 1/2 tsp (1g, 0.04 oz),
- Fresh parsley: 2 tbsp, chopped (10g, 0.35 oz),
- Salt: to taste,
- Parmesan cheese: for serving (optional)

 Calories: 400 kcal,
Carbohydrates: 55 g, Protein: 10 g, Fat: 15 g (Saturated Fat: 2 g, Monounsaturated Fat: 10 g, Polyunsaturated Fat: 1 g), Cholesterol: 0 mg, Sodium: 200 mg, Fiber: 3 g, Sugars: 2 g

 Interesting Fact: This classic Italian dish, also known as "Spaghetti Aglio e Olio," is loved for its simplicity and rich flavor, making it a staple in Italian cuisine.

 Chef's Tips: "Use high-quality olive oil for the best flavor."

Instructions

- **Preparation:** Cook spaghetti according to package instructions until al dente. Drain and set aside.
- **Cooking:** Heat olive oil in a large skillet over medium heat. Add garlic and red pepper flakes, cook until garlic is golden brown, about 2 min. Add cooked spaghetti to the skillet, tossing to coat in the garlic oil.
- **Assembly:** Mix in fresh parsley and season with salt.
- **Serving:** Serve hot, topped with grated Parmesan cheese if desired.

57 Eggplant Parmesan

 Country of Origin: Italy

 Prep: 20 mins | **Cook:** 40 mins | **Total:** 1 hr | **Level:** 3/5 | **Servings:** 2

Ingredients

- Eggplant: 1 large, sliced (500g, 17.64 oz),
- Salt: to taste, Olive oil: 2 tbsp (30ml, 1.01 oz),
- Marinara sauce: 2 cups (480ml, 16.91 oz),
- Mozzarella cheese: 1 cup, shredded (100g, 3.53 oz),
- Parmesan cheese: 1/2 cup, grated (50g, 1.76 oz),
- Fresh basil: 1/4 cup, chopped (10g, 0.35 oz),
- Bread crumbs: 1 cup (120g, 4.23 oz)

Instructions

- **Preparation:** Preheat the oven to 375°F (190°C). Slice eggplant and sprinkle it with salt. Let sit for 10 min to draw out moisture, then pat dry.
- **Cooking:** Heat olive oil in a skillet over medium heat. Fry eggplant slices until golden, about 3 min per side. In a baking dish, layer marinara sauce, eggplant slices, mozzarella, Parmesan, and basil. Repeat layers. Top with bread crumbs.
- **Assembly:** Ensure even layering of ingredients.
- **Serving:** Bake for 30 min until bubbly and golden. Serve hot.

 Chef's Tips: "Serve with a side of spaghetti or a fresh green salad."

 Calories: 450 kcal,
Carbohydrates: 40 g, Protein: 20 g, Fat: 25 g (Saturated Fat: 10 g, Monounsaturated Fat: 12 g, Polyunsaturated Fat: 2 g), Cholesterol: 50 mg, Sodium: 800 mg, Fiber: 8 g, Sugars: 10 g

 Interesting Fact: Eggplant Parmesan, or "Melanzane alla Parmigiana," is a classic Italian dish loved for its rich flavors and comforting textures.

58 Grilled Lamb Chops with Herbs

 Country of Origin: Mediterranean Region

Prep: 15 mins | **Cook:** 15 mins | **Total:** 25 mins | **Level:** 2/5 | **Servings:** 2

Ingredients

- Lamb chops: 4 (400g, 14.11 oz),
- Olive oil: 2 tbsp (30ml, 1.01 oz),
- Fresh rosemary: 2 tbsp, chopped (10g, 0.35 oz),
- Fresh thyme: 2 tbsp, chopped (10g, 0.35 oz),
- Garlic: 3 cloves, minced (9g, 0.32 oz),
- Lemon zest: 1 tbsp (6g, 0.21 oz),
- Salt and pepper: to taste

Instructions

- **Preparation:** Preheat grill to medium-high heat. In a bowl, mix olive oil, rosemary, thyme, garlic, lemon zest, salt, and pepper.
- **Cooking:** Rub the herb mixture onto the lamb chops. Grill for 6-7 min per side until desired doneness.
- **Assembly:** Let the lamb chops rest for 5 min.
- **Serving:** Serve hot, garnished with additional fresh herbs if desired.

 Calories: 450 kcal,
Carbohydrates: 2 g, Protein: 40 g, Fat: 30 g (Saturated Fat: 10 g, Monounsaturated Fat: 15 g, Polyunsaturated Fat: 2 g), Cholesterol: 120 mg, Sodium: 400 mg, Fiber: 1 g, Sugars: 1 g

 Interesting Fact: Lamb chops are a popular dish in Mediterranean cuisine, often enjoyed for their rich flavor and tender texture.

 Chef's Tips: "Pair with a side of roasted vegetables or a fresh salad."

59 Ratatouille

 Country of Origin: France

Prep: 15 mins | **Cook:** 45 mins | **Total:** 60 mins | **Level:** 2/5 | **Servings:** 2

Ingredients

- Eggplant: 1, diced (300g, 10.58 oz),
- Zucchini: 1, diced (200g, 7.05 oz),
- Red Bell pepper: 1, diced (120g, 4.23 oz),
- Onion: 1, chopped (150g, 5.29 oz),
- Garlic: 3 cloves, minced (9g, 0.32 oz),
- Tomatoes: 2, chopped (300g, 10.58 oz),
- Olive oil: 3 tbsp (45ml, 1.52 oz),
- Fresh thyme: 1 tsp (1g, 0.04 oz),
- Fresh basil: 1/4 cup, chopped (10g, 0.35 oz),
- Salt and pepper: to taste

Instructions

- **Preparation:** Dice eggplant, zucchini, bell pepper, and tomatoes. Chop onion and mince garlic.
- **Cooking:** Heat olive oil in a large pot over medium heat. Sauté onion and garlic for 5 min. Add eggplant, zucchini, and bell pepper, cook for 10 min. Stir in tomatoes, thyme, salt, and pepper. Simmer for 30 min, stirring occasionally.
- **Assembly:** Mix in fresh basil before serving.
- **Serving:** Serve hot or at room temperature, garnished with additional basil if desired.

 Chef's Tips: "Serve with crusty bread or as a side to grilled meats."

 Calories: 200 kcal,
Carbohydrates: 25 g, Protein: 4 g, Fat: 10 g (Saturated Fat: 1.5 g, Monounsaturated Fat: 6 g, Polyunsaturated Fat: 1 g), Cholesterol: 0 mg, Sodium: 400 mg, Fiber: 7 g, Sugars: 12 g

 Interesting Fact: Ratatouille is a traditional Provençal dish that highlights the rich flavors of summer vegetables, making it a staple in French cuisine.

60

Saffron Rice with Vegetables

Country of Origin:

Mediterranean Region

 Prep: 10 mins | **Cook:** 25 mins | **Total:** 35 mins | **Level:** 2/5 | **Servings:** 2

Ingredients

- Basmati rice: 1 cup (200g),
- Olive oil: 2 tbsp (30ml),
- Onion: 1, chopped (150g),
- Carrot: 1, diced (60g),
- Bell pepper: 1, diced (120g),
- Green peas: 1/2 cup (75g),
- Garlic: 2 cloves, minced (6g),
- Saffron threads: 1/2 tsp (0.5g),
- Vegetable broth: 2 cups (480ml),
- Fresh parsley: 1/4 cup, chopped (10g),
- Salt and pepper: to taste

 Calories: 350 kcal,
Carbohydrates: 60 g, Protein: 6 g, Fat: 10 g (Saturated Fat: 1.5 g, Monounsaturated Fat: 6 g, Polyunsaturated Fat: 1 g), Cholesterol: 0 mg, Sodium: 500 mg, Fiber: 4 g, Sugars: 5 g

 Interesting Fact: Saffron, known as the world's most expensive spice, adds a unique flavor and vibrant color to dishes, making it a prized ingredient in Mediterranean cooking.

 Chef's Tips: "For added flavor, toast the saffron threads lightly before adding them to the dish."

Instructions

- **Preparation:** Rinse rice. Chop onion, carrot, and bell pepper. Mince garlic.
- **Cooking:** Heat olive oil, sauté onion and garlic for 5 min. Add carrot, bell pepper, cook for 5 min. Stir in rice, saffron, and broth. Simmer for 20 min. Add peas for the last 5 min.
- **Assembly:** Fluff rice, mix in parsley. Season with salt and pepper.
- **Serving:** Serve hot, garnish with parsley.

61

Shrimp and Vegetable Stir Fry

Country of Origin:
Mediterranean Region

 Prep: 10 mins | **Cook:** 10 mins |  **Total:** 20 mins | **Level:** 2/5 | **Servings:** 2

Ingredients

- Shrimp: 200g (7.05 oz),
- Olive oil: 2 tbsp (30ml),
- Red or yellow bell pepper: 1, sliced (120g),
- Zucchini: 1, sliced (150g),
- Carrot: 1, julienned (60g),
- Garlic: 2 cloves, minced (6g),
- Soy sauce: 2 tbsp (30ml),
- Lemon juice: 1 tbsp (15ml),
- Fresh parsley: 2 tbsp, chopped (10g),
- Salt and pepper: to taste

Instructions

- **Preparation:** Slice bell pepper, zucchini, carrot. Mince garlic.
- **Cooking:** Heat olive oil in a skillet. Sauté garlic for 1 min. Add shrimp, cook 2 min per side. Add bell pepper, zucchini, carrot, cook for 5 min. Stir in soy sauce and lemon juice, cook for 2 min.
- **Assembly:** Mix in fresh parsley. Season with salt and pepper.
- **Serving:** Serve hot, garnish with additional parsley.

 Chef's Tips: "Serve over quinoa or brown rice for a complete meal."

 Calories: 300 kcal,
Carbohydrates: 15 g, Protein: 25 g, Fat: 15 g (Saturated Fat: 2 g, Monounsaturated Fat: 9 g, Polyunsaturated Fat: 2 g), Fiber: 4 g, Sugars: 5 g

 Interesting Fact: Stir-frying is a quick and healthy cooking method that preserves the nutrients and flavors of fresh vegetables.

62 Chicken Marsala

Country of Origin: Italy

Prep: 10 mins | **Cook:** 20 mins | **Total:** 30 mins | **Level:** 2/5 | **Servings:** 2

Ingredients

- Chicken breasts: 2 (300g),
- Olive oil: 2 tbsp (30ml),
- Butter: 1 tbsp (15g),
- Mushrooms: 1 cup, sliced (150g),
- Garlic: 2 cloves, minced (6g),
- Marsala wine: 1/2 cup (120ml),
- Chicken broth: 1/2 cup (120ml),
- Fresh parsley: 2 tbsp, chopped (10g),
- Salt and pepper: to taste

Instructions

- **Preparation:** Slice mushrooms and minced garlic.
- **Cooking:** Heat olive oil and butter in a skillet. Cook chicken 5 min per side. Remove chicken, add mushrooms and garlic, cook for 5 min. Add Marsala wine and broth, simmer for 5 min. Return chicken, cook for 5 min.
- **Assembly:** Mix in fresh parsley. Season with salt and pepper.
- **Serving:** Serve hot, garnish with additional parsley.

Calories: 400 kcal,
Carbohydrates: 10 g, Protein: 35 g, Fat: 20 g (Saturated Fat: 5 g, Monounsaturated Fat: 10 g, Polyunsaturated Fat: 3 g), Fiber: 2 g, Sugars: 3 g

Interesting Fact: Chicken Marsala is a classic Italian-American dish that combines the rich flavors of Marsala wine and mushrooms.

Chef's Tips: "Pair with mashed potatoes or pasta."

63 Pesto Pasta with Cherry Tomatoes

Country of Origin: Italy

Prep: 15 mins | **Cook:** 10 mins | **Total:** 25 mins | **Level:** 2/5 | **Servings:** 2

Instructions

- **Preparation:** Cook the pasta in salted water according to package instructions. While the pasta cooks, halve the cherry tomatoes.
- **Cooking** (Pesto Sauce): In a food processor, combine the basil leaves, pine nuts, Parmesan, and garlic. Pulse until the ingredients are finely chopped. With the processor running, slowly drizzle in the olive oil until the mixture becomes smooth. Add lemon juice and salt to taste.
- **Assembly:** Once the pasta is cooked and drained, toss it with the pesto sauce and halved cherry tomatoes.
- **Serving:** Plate the pesto pasta and garnish with extra Parmesan if desired. Serve immediately.

Calories: 500 kcal,
Carbohydrates: 55 g, Protein: 12 g, Fat: 28 g (Saturated Fat: 5 g, Monounsaturated Fat: 18 g, Polyunsaturated Fat: 3 g), Cholesterol: 10 mg, Sodium: 150 mg, Fiber: 8 g, Sugars: 5 g

Ingredients

- Pasta (whole grain or your choice): 200g (7.05 oz),
- Cherry tomatoes: 1 cup (150g, 5.29 oz),
- Olive oil: 1 tbsp (15ml, 0.51 oz),
- Parmesan cheese (optional): 2 tbsp, grated (30g, 1.06 oz),
- Salt and pepper: to taste

For Pesto Sauce

- Fresh basil leaves: 2cups (60g),
- Olive oil: 1/3 cup (80ml),
- Pine nuts: 1/4 cup (35g),
- Parmesan cheese: 1/4cup (30g),
- Garlic: 2 cloves, minced (6g),
- Lemon juice: 1 tbsp (15ml),
- Salt: to taste

Interesting Fact: Pesto sauce originates from Genoa, Italy, and the word "pesto" comes from the Italian word "pestare," meaning to crush or pound, referring to the traditional method of making pesto with a mortar and pestle.

Chef's Tips: "For a creamier pesto, add a spoonful of Greek yogurt or a splash of cream to the sauce."

64 Baked Cod with Vegetables

Country of Origin: Mediterranean Region

Prep: 10 mins | **Cook:** 20 mins | **Total:** 30 mins | **Level:** 2/5 | **Servings:** 2

Ingredients

- Cod fillets: 2 (300g),
- Olive oil: 2 tbsp (30ml),
- Cherry tomatoes: 1 cup, halved (150g),
- Zucchini: 1, sliced (150g),
- Bell pepper: 1, sliced (120g),
- Red onion: 1, sliced (150g),
- Garlic: 2 cloves, minced (6g),
- Lemon: 1, sliced (120g),
- Fresh thyme: 2 tsp (2g),
- Salt and pepper: to taste

Calories: 350 kcal,
Carbohydrates: 20 g, Protein: 35 g, Fat: 15 g (Saturated Fat: 2.5 g, Monounsaturated Fat: 9 g, Polyunsaturated Fat: 2 g), Fiber: 6 g, Sugars: 8 g

Interesting Fact: Cod is a lean, protein-rich fish often used in Mediterranean cuisine for its mild flavor and versatility in various dishes.

Chef's Tips: "Serve with a side of couscous or quinoa for a complete meal."

Instructions

- **Preparation:** Preheat the oven to 375ºF (190ºC). Halve cherry tomatoes, slice zucchini, bell pepper, red onion, and lemon. Mince garlic.
- **Cooking:** Place cod fillets on a baking sheet. Arrange vegetables and lemon slices around the cod. Drizzle with olive oil, sprinkle with garlic, thyme, salt, and pepper. Bake for 20 min until cod is cooked through and vegetables are tender.
- **Assembly:** Ensure even distribution of vegetables around the cod fillets.
- **Serving:** Serve hot, garnished with additional fresh thyme if desired.

65 Feta Stuffed Peppers

Country of Origin: Greece

Prep: 15 mins | **Cook:** 25 mins | **Total:** 40 mins | **Level:** 2/5 | **Servings:** 2

Ingredients

- Red or yellow bell peppers: 2, halved and seeded (240g),
- Feta cheese: 1 cup, crumbled (150g),
- Olive oil: 2 tbsp (30ml),
- Cherry tomatoes: 1/2 cup, diced (75g),
- Red onion: 1/4 cup, finely chopped (37g),
- Fresh parsley: 2 tbsp, chopped (10g),
- Fresh basil: 2 tbsp, chopped (10g),
- Garlic: 2 cloves, minced (6g),
- Lemon zest: 1 tsp (2g),
- Salt and pepper: to taste

Instructions

- **Preparation:** Preheat the oven to 375ºF (190ºC). Halve and seed bell peppers. Dice cherry tomatoes and finely chop red onion. Mince garlic.
- **Cooking:** In a bowl, mix feta, olive oil, cherry tomatoes, red onion, parsley, basil, garlic, lemon zest, salt, and pepper. Stuffed pepper halves with the mixture. Place stuffed peppers on a baking sheet and bake for 25 min until peppers are tender and cheese is golden.
- **Assembly:** Ensure stuffing is evenly distributed in the pepper halves.
- **Serving:** Serve hot, garnished with additional fresh herbs if desired.

Chef's Tips: "Pair with a fresh Greek salad for a complete meal."

Calories: 300 kcal,
Carbohydrates: 10 g, Protein: 12 g, Fat: 25 g (Saturated Fat: 8 g, Monounsaturated Fat: 12 g, Polyunsaturated Fat: 3 g), Fiber: 3 g, Sugars: 6 g

Interesting Fact: Stuffed peppers are a versatile dish enjoyed throughout the Mediterranean, with each region adding its own twist of flavors and ingredients.

66 Lentil Soup with Spinach

Country of Origin: Mediterranean Region

Prep: 10 mins | **Cook:** 30 mins | **Total:** 40 mins | **Level:** 2/5 | **Servings:** 2

Ingredients

- Green lentils: 1 cup (200g),
- Olive oil: 2 tbsp (30ml),
- Onion: 1, chopped (150g),
- Carrot: 1, diced (60g),
- Celery: 2 stalks, diced (100g),
- Garlic: 2 cloves, minced (6g),
- Vegetable broth: 4 cups (960ml),
- Canned tomatoes: 1 cup (240g),
- Fresh spinach: 2 cups (60g),
- Cumin: 1 tsp (2g),
- Salt and pepper: to taste

Instructions

- **Preparation:** Rinse lentils. Chop onion, carrot, celery, and minced garlic.
- **Cooking:** Heat olive oil in a pot over medium heat. Sauté onion, carrot, and celery for 5 min. Add garlic, cook for 1 min. Add lentils, broth, tomatoes, cumin, salt, and pepper. Bring to a boil, reduce heat, simmer for 25 min. Stir in spinach, cook for 5 min.
- **Assembly:** Mix well to combine all ingredients.
- **Serving:** Serve hot, garnished with fresh herbs if desired.

Calories: 350 kcal,
Carbohydrates: 50 g, Protein: 18 g, Fat: 10 g (Saturated Fat: 1.5 g, Monounsaturated Fat: 6 g, Polyunsaturated Fat: 2 g), Fiber: 15 g, Sugars: 8 g

Interesting Fact: Lentil soup is a staple in Mediterranean cuisine, known for its hearty and nutritious properties, making it a perfect comfort food.

Chef's Tips: "Add a squeeze of lemon juice before serving for extra brightness."

67 Roasted Cauliflower with Tahini

Country of Origin: Mediterranean Region

Prep: 10 mins | **Cook:** 25 mins | **Total:** 35 mins | **Level:** 1/5 | **Servings:** 2

Ingredients

- Cauliflower: 1 head, cut into florets (500g),
- Olive oil: 2 tbsp (30ml),
- Tahini: 1/4 cup (60g),
- Lemon juice: 2 tbsp (30ml),
- Garlic: 2 cloves, minced (6g),
- Water: 2 tbsp (30ml),
- Salt and pepper: to taste,
- Fresh parsley: 2 tbsp, chopped (10g)

Chef's Tips: "Add a sprinkle of smoked paprika for extra flavor."

Calories: 250 kcal,
Carbohydrates: 15 g, Protein: 7 g, Fat: 18 g (Saturated Fat: 2.5 g, Monounsaturated Fat: 10 g, Polyunsaturated Fat: 3 g), Fiber: 7 g, Sugars: 5 g

Interesting Fact: Tahini, made from ground sesame seeds, is a staple in Mediterranean cuisine, adding a rich, nutty flavor to dishes.

Instructions

- **Preparation:** Preheat the oven to 400°F (200°C). Cut cauliflower into florets.
- **Cooking:** Toss cauliflower with olive oil, salt, and pepper. Spread on a baking sheet. Roast for 25 min until golden. In a bowl, mix tahini, lemon juice, garlic, water, salt, and pepper.
- **Assembly:** Drizzle tahini sauce over roasted cauliflower.
- **Serving:** Serve hot, garnished with fresh parsley.

68 Moroccan Chicken with Apricots

 Country of Origin:
Morocco

 Prep: 15 mins | **Cook:** 45 mins | **Total:** 1hr | **Level:** 3/5 | **Servings:** 2

Ingredients

- Chicken thighs: 4 (400g),
- Olive oil: 2 tbsp (30ml),
- Onion: 1, chopped (150g),
- Garlic: 3 cloves, minced (9g),
- Dried apricots: 1/2 cup, chopped (75g),
- Chicken broth: 1 cup (240ml),
- Honey: 1 tbsp (21g),
- Ground cumin: 1 tsp (2g),
- Ground cinnamon: 1/2 tsp (1g),
- Ground ginger: 1/2 tsp (1g),
- Salt and pepper: to taste,
- Fresh cilantro: 2 tbsp, chopped (10g)

 Calories: 500 kcal,
Carbohydrates: 40 g, Protein: 30 g, Fat: 25 g (Saturated Fat: 6 g, Monounsaturated Fat: 14 g, Polyunsaturated Fat: 2 g), Fiber: 5 g, Sugars: 25 g

 Interesting Fact: Moroccan cuisine often combines sweet and savory flavors, as seen in this dish, which pairs tender chicken with sweet apricots and aromatic spices.

 Chef's Tips: "Serve with couscous or rice to soak up the flavorful sauce."

Instructions

- **Preparation:** Chop onion, garlic, and apricots.
- **Cooking:** Heat olive oil in a pot over medium heat. Brown chicken thighs on both sides, remove. In the same pot, sauté onion and garlic for 5 min. Add apricots, broth, honey, cumin, cinnamon, ginger, salt, and pepper. Return chicken to the pot, simmer for 35 min.
- **Assembly:** Ensure chicken is cooked through and sauce is thickened.
- **Serving:** Serve hot, garnished with fresh cilantro.

69 Vegetable Paella

 Country of Origin:
Spain

 Prep: 15 mins | **Cook:** 40 mins | **Total:** 55 mins | **Level:** 3/5 | **Servings:** 2

Ingredients

- Short-grain rice: 1 cup (200g),
- Vegetable broth: 3 cups (720ml),
- Saffron threads: 1/2 tsp (0.5g),
- Paprika: 1 tsp (2g),
- Salt and pepper: to taste,
- Lemon wedges: for serving,
- Fresh parsley: for garnish
- Olive oil: 2 tbsp (30ml),
- Onion: 1, chopped (150g),
- Garlic: 2 cloves, minced (6g),
- Bell pepper: 1, diced (120g),
- Tomato: 1, chopped (150g),
- Green beans: 1/2 cup (75g),
- Peas: 1/2 cup (75g),
- Artichoke hearts: 1/2 cup, quartered (75g),

Instructions

- **Preparation:** Chop onion, bell pepper, tomato, and artichoke hearts. Mince garlic.
- **Cooking:** Heat olive oil in a large skillet over medium heat. Sauté onion and garlic for 5 min. Add bell pepper, tomato, green beans, peas, and artichoke hearts. Cook for 5 min. Stir in rice, saffron, and paprika. Add vegetable broth, bring to a boil, reduce heat, simmer for 25 min until rice is tender.
- **Assembly:** Ensure all ingredients are evenly distributed and rice is fully cooked.
- **Serving:** Serve hot, garnished with fresh parsley and lemon wedges.

 Chef's Tips: "For added flavor, grill the vegetables before adding them to the paella."

 Calories: 400 kcal,
Carbohydrates: 70 g, Protein: 8 g, Fat: 10 g (Saturated Fat: 1.5 g, Monounsaturated Fat: 6 g, Polyunsaturated Fat: 2 g), Fiber: 8 g, Sugars: 10 g

Interesting Fact: Paella is a traditional Spanish dish originally from Valencia, known for its vibrant flavors and versatility, often featuring a variety of seasonal vegetables and spices.

70 Greek Moussaka

 **Country of Origin:** Greece

 Prep: 20 mins | **Cook:** 45 mins | **Total:** 1hr 5 mins | **Level:** 3/5 | **Servings:** 2

Ingredients

- Eggplant: 1 large, sliced (300g),
- Ground beef: 200g (7.05 oz),
- Olive oil: 3 tbsp (45ml),
- Onion: 1, chopped (150Rg),
- Garlic: 2 cloves, minced (6g),
- Tomatoes: 2, chopped (300g),
- Tomato paste: 2 tbsp (30g),
- Red wine: 1/4 cup (60ml),
- Fresh parsley: 2 tbsp, chopped (10g),
- Salt and pepper: to taste,
- Béchamel sauce: 1 cup (240ml),
- Parmesan cheese: 1/4 cup, grated (30g)

Instructions

- **Preparation:** Slice eggplant and sprinkle it with salt. Let sit for 10 min to remove bitterness, then pat dry.
- **Cooking:** Heat olive oil in a skillet, cook eggplant slices until golden. In another pan, cook ground beef, onion, and garlic until beef is browned. Add tomatoes, tomato paste, wine, parsley, salt, and pepper. Simmer for 20 min. Layer eggplant and meat sauce in a baking dish. Top with béchamel sauce and grated Parmesan. Bake at 375°F (190°C) for 25 min until golden.
- **Assembly:** Ensure even layering of eggplant and meat sauce.
- **Serving:** Serve hot, garnished with fresh parsley.

 Calories: 600 kcal,
Carbohydrates: 30 g, Protein: 25 g, Fat: 40 g (Saturated Fat: 10 g, Monounsaturated Fat: 20 g, Polyunsaturated Fat: 5 g), Fiber: 6 g, Sugars: 12 g

 Interesting Fact: Moussaka is a beloved Greek dish, known for its rich layers of eggplant, meat sauce, and creamy béchamel, often enjoyed as a comforting family meal.

 Chef's Tips: "Let the moussaka sit for a few minutes before serving to allow the flavors to meld."

71 Herbed Quinoa with Chickpeas

 Country of Origin: Mediterranean Region

 Prep: 10 mins | **Cook:** 15 mins | **Total:** 25 mins | **Level:** 1/5 | **Servings:** 2

Ingredients

- Quinoa: 1 cup (200g),
- Chickpeas: 1 cup, cooked (240g),
- Olive oil: 2 tbsp (30ml),
- Lemon juice: 2 tbsp (30ml),
- Fresh parsley: 1/4 cup, chopped (10g),
- Fresh mint: 2 tbsp, chopped (5g),
- Garlic: 1 clove, minced (3g),
- Cumin: 1 tsp (2g),
- Salt and pepper: to taste

Instructions

- **Preparation:** Rinse quinoa. Mince garlic and chop parsley and mint.
- **Cooking:** Cook quinoa according to package instructions. In a bowl, mix olive oil, lemon juice, garlic, cumin, salt, and pepper. Stir in chickpeas and cooked quinoa.
- **Assembly:** Mix in fresh herbs. Adjust seasoning as needed.
- **Serving:** Serve warm or cold, garnished with additional herbs if desired.

 Chef's Tips: "Add diced cucumbers and tomatoes for extra freshness."

 Calories: 350 kcal,
Carbohydrates: 50 g, Protein: 12 g, Fat: 12g (Saturated Fat: 1.5g, Monoun- saturated Fat: 7 g, Polyunsaturated Fat: 2 g), Fiber: 10 g, Sugars: 3 g

 Interesting Fact: Quinoa, a staple in Mediterranean cuisine, is a protein-rich grain that pairs perfectly with chickpeas for a nutritious and flavorful dish.

Roasted Brussels Sprouts with Garlic

 Country of Origin: Mediterranean Region

 Prep: 10 mins **Cook:** 25 mins **Total:** 35 mins **Level:** 1/5 **Servings:** 2

Ingredients

- Brussels sprouts: 500g,
- Olive oil: 2 tbsp (30ml),
- Garlic: 3 cloves, minced (9g),
- Lemon juice: 1 tbsp (15ml),
- Salt and pepper: to taste,
- Fresh parsley: 2 tbsp, chopped (10g)

Instructions

- **Preparation:** Halve Brussels sprouts and mince garlic.
- **Cooking:** Heat olive oil in a large skillet over medium-high heat. Add Brussels sprouts, cut side down, and cook for 5-7 minutes until golden brown. Add minced garlic and cook for another 2-3 minutes, stirring occasionally. Season with salt and pepper.
- **Assembly:** Drizzle with lemon juice and mix in fresh parsley.
- **Serving:** Serve hot, garnished with additional parsley if desired.

 Calories: 200 kcal, Carbohydrates: 20 g, Protein: 6 g, Fat: 12 g (Saturated Fat: 1.5 g, Monounsaturated Fat: 7 g, Polyunsaturated Fat: 2 g), Fiber: 8 g, Sugars: 4 g

 Interesting Fact: Brussels sprouts, rich in vitamins and fiber, are a popular vegetable in Mediterranean diets, often enjoyed roasted to bring out their natural sweetness.

 Chef's Tips: "Add a sprinkle of grated Parmesan for extra flavor."

Tabbouleh Salad with Fresh Herbs

 Country of Origin: Lebanon

 Prep: 15 mins **Cook:** 0 mins **Total:** 15 mins **Level:** 1/5 **Servings:** 2

Ingredients

- Bulgur wheat: 1/2 cup (90g),
- Hot water: 1 cup (240ml),
- Fresh parsley: 1 cup, finely chopped (50g),
- Fresh mint: 1/4 cup, finely chopped (10g),
- Tomatoes: 2, diced (300g),
- Cucumber: 1, diced (150g),
- Green onions: 2, sliced (30g),
- Olive oil: 2 tbsp (30ml),
- Lemon juice: 2 tbsp (30ml),
- Salt and pepper: to taste

Instructions

- **Preparation:** Soak bulgur in hot water for 10 min, drain excess water. Finely chop parsley and mint. Dice tomatoes and cucumber, slice green onions.
- **Assembly:** In a large bowl, combine bulgur, parsley, mint, tomatoes, cucumber, and green onions. Add olive oil, lemon juice, salt, and pepper. Toss to combine.
- **Serving:** Serve cold, garnished with additional fresh herbs if desired.

 Chef's Tips: "For extra flavor, add a pinch of ground cinnamon."

 Calories: 220 kcal, Carbohydrates: 30 g, Protein: 4 g, Fat: 10 g (Saturated Fat: 1.5 g, Monounsaturated Fat: 7 g, Polyunsaturated Fat: 1 g), Fiber: 8 g, Sugars: 6 g

 Interesting Fact: Tabbouleh is a classic Lebanese salad known for its fresh and vibrant flavors, making it a popular dish in Mediterranean cuisine.

74 Greek Chicken Gyros

Country of Origin: Greece

 Prep: 20 mins | Cook: 45 mins | Total: 1hr 5 mins | Level: 3/5 | Servings: 2

Ingredients

- Chicken breasts: 2 (300g),
- Greek yogurt: 1/2 cup (120g),
- Olive oil: 2 tbsp (30ml),
- Lemon juice: 2 tbsp (30ml),
- Garlic: 3 cloves, minced (9g),
- Dried oregano: 1 tsp (2g),
- Salt and pepper: to taste,
- Pita bread: 2,
- Cucumber: 1, sliced (150g),
- Tomato: 1, sliced (150g),
- Red onion: 1/2, sliced (75g),
- Fresh dill: 2 tbs
- Paprika: 1 tsp (2g), p, chopped (10g)

Instructions

- **Preparation:** Slice cucumber, tomato, and red onion. Mince garlic.
- **Cooking:** In a bowl, mix Greek yogurt, olive oil, lemon juice, garlic, oregano, paprika, salt, and pepper. Add chicken, marinate for 15 min. Grill chicken for 5-7 min per side until cooked through. Slice chicken into strips.
- **Assembly:** Warm pita bread. Fill each pita with sliced chicken, cucumber, tomato, red onion, and fresh dill.
- **Serving:** Serve hot, optionally with a side of tzatziki sauce.

Calories: 450 kcal,
Carbohydrates: 35 g, Protein: 35 g, Fat: 18 g (Saturated Fat: 4 g, Monounsaturated Fat: 10 g, Polyunsaturated Fat: 2 g), Fiber: 4 g, Sugars: 6 g

Interesting Fact: Gyros, a popular Greek street food, are traditionally made with pork or chicken and served in pita bread with fresh vegetables and yogurt-based sauces.

Chef's Tips: "For extra flavor, let the chicken marinate overnight."

75 Spinach and Feta Pie

Country of Origin: Greece

 Prep: 20 mins | Cook: 40 mins | Total: 1 hr | Level: 3/5 | Servings: 2

Ingredients

- Fresh spinach: 500g,
- Olive oil: 2 tbsp (30ml),
- Onion: 1, chopped (150g),
- Garlic: 2 cloves, minced (6g),
- Feta cheese: 1 cup, crumbled (150g),
- Fresh dill: 2 tbsp, chopped (10g),
- Phyllo dough: 6 sheets,
- Eggs: 2, beaten,
- Salt and pepper: to taste

Instructions

- **Preparation:** Preheat the oven to 375°F (190°C). Chop onion and mince garlic.
- **Cooking:** Sauté onion and garlic in olive oil until soft. Add spinach, cook until wilted. Remove from heat, stir in feta, dill, salt, and pepper. Brush a baking dish with olive oil. Layer 3 sheets of phyllo, brushing each with olive oil. Add spinach mixture, top with remaining phyllo, brushing each sheet with olive oil. Brush top with beaten eggs. Bake for 40 min until golden.
- **Assembly:** Ensure phyllo sheets are evenly layered.
- **Serving:** Let cool slightly before serving.

Chef's Tips: "For a crispier crust, use more phyllo sheets."

Calories: 400 kcal,
Carbohydrates: 30 g, Protein: 18 g, Fat: 24 g (Saturated Fat: 8 g, Monounsaturated Fat: 12 g, Polyunsaturated Fat: 2 g), Fiber: 5 g, Sugars: 6 g

Interesting Fact: Spanakopita, a traditional Greek dish, is a savory pie filled with spinach, feta, and herbs, often enjoyed as a main dish or appetizer.

76 Grilled Vegetable Skewers

Country of Origin:
Mediterranean Region

 Prep: 15 mins | **Cook**: 10 mins | **Total**: 25 mins | **Level**: 1/5 | **Servings**: 2

Ingredients

- Bell peppers: 2, cut into chunks (240g),
- Zucchini: 1, sliced (150g),
- Cherry tomatoes: 1 cup (150g),
- Red onion: 1, cut into chunks (150g),
- Olive oil: 2 tbsp (30ml),
- Lemon juice: 1 tbsp (15ml),
- Garlic: 2 cloves, minced (6g),
- Dried oregano: 1 tsp (2g),
- Salt and pepper: to taste

Instructions

- **Preparation:** Cut vegetables into chunks. Mince garlic.
- **Cooking:** In a bowl, mix olive oil, lemon juice, garlic, oregano, salt, and pepper. Toss vegetables in the mixture. Thread vegetables onto skewers. Grill over medium heat for 8-10 min, turning occasionally, until vegetables are tender and slightly charred.
- **Assembly:** Ensure even distribution of vegetables on skewers.
- **Serving:** Serve hot, optionally with a side of tzatziki sauce.

 Calories: 180 kcal,
Carbohydrates: 25 g, Protein: 4 g, Fat: 10 g (Saturated Fat: 1.5 g, Monounsaturated Fat: 6 g, Polyunsaturated Fat: 2 g), Fiber: 6 g, Sugars: 10 g

 Interesting Fact: Grilled vegetable skewers are a popular Mediterranean dish, offering a healthy and colorful way to enjoy a variety of seasonal vegetables.

 Chef's Tips: "For added flavor, marinate the vegetables for 30 minutes before grilling"

77 Stuffed Zucchini Boats

Country of Origin:
Mediterranean Region

 Prep: 15 mins | **Cook**: 25 mins | **Total**: 40 mins | **Level**: 2/5 | **Servings**: 2

Ingredients

- Zucchini: 2 large, halved and scooped out (300g),
- Ground beef or turkey: 200g,
- Olive oil: 2 tbsp (30ml),
- Onion: 1, chopped (150g),
- Garlic: 2 cloves, minced (6g),
- Tomato sauce: 1 cup (240ml),
- Parmesan cheese: 1/4 cup, grated (30g),
- Fresh parsley: 2 tbsp, chopped (10g),
- Salt and pepper: to taste

Instructions

- **Preparation:** Preheat the oven to 375ºF (190ºC). Halve zucchinis and scoop out centers. Chop onion and mince garlic.
- **Cooking:** Heat olive oil in a skillet. Sauté onion and garlic until soft. Add ground meat, cook until browned. Stir in tomato sauce, salt, and pepper. Fill zucchini halves with the mixture, top with grated Parmesan. Place in a baking dish and bake for 25 min.
- **Assembly:** Ensure even distribution of filling in zucchini halves.
- **Serving:** Serve hot, garnished with fresh parsley.

 Chef's Tips: "For extra flavor, add a pinch of ground cinnamon."

 Calories: 350 kcal,
Carbohydrates: 15 g, Protein: 25 g, Fat: 20 g (Saturated Fat: 5 g, Monounsaturated Fat: 10 g, Polyunsaturated Fat: 3 g), Fiber: 5 g, Sugars: 8 g

 Interesting Fact: Stuffed zucchini boats are a versatile Mediterranean dish that can be customized with various fillings, making it a popular choice for using seasonal vegetables.

78 Baked Eggplant with Tomatoes and Feta

 Country of Origin: Greece

 Prep: 15 mins | **Cook:** 30 mins | **Total:** 45 mins | **Level:** 2/5 | **Servings:** 2

Ingredients

- Eggplant: 1 large, sliced (300g),
- Olive oil: 2 tbsp (30ml),
- Tomatoes: 2, sliced (300g),
- Feta cheese: 1/2 cup, crumbled (75g),
- Garlic: 2 cloves, minced (6g),
- Fresh basil: 2 tbsp, chopped (10g),
- Salt and pepper: to taste

Instructions

- **Preparation:** Preheat the oven to 375ºF (190ºC). Slice eggplant and tomatoes. Mince garlic.
- **Cooking:** Brush eggplant slices with olive oil, season with salt and pepper. Arrange in a baking dish. Layer tomatoes on top. Sprinkle with minced garlic and crumbled feta. Bake for 30 min until eggplant is tender and cheese is golden.
- **Assembly:** Ensure even layering of eggplant, tomatoes, and feta.
- **Serving:** Serve hot, garnished with fresh basil.

 Calories: 300 kcal,
Carbohydrates: 20 g, Protein: 8 g, Fat: 22 g (Saturated Fat: 6 g, Monounsaturated Fat: 12 g, Polyunsaturated Fat: 2 g), Fiber: 8 g, Sugars: 10 g

 Interesting Fact: Baked eggplant with tomatoes and feta is a classic Greek dish, showcasing the rich flavors of Mediterranean vegetables and cheese.

 Chef's Tips: "For extra flavor, drizzle with balsamic vinegar before serving."

79 Mediterranean Meatloaf

 **Country of Origin:** Mediterranean Region

 Prep: 15 mins | **Cook:** 1 hr | **Total:** 1 hr 15 mins | **Level:** 3/5 | **Servings:** 2

Ingredients

- Ground beef: 200g,
- Ground lamb: 200g,
- Olive oil: 2 tbsp (30ml),
- Onion: 1, chopped (150g),
- Garlic: 2 cloves, minced (6g),
- Feta cheese: 1/2 cup, crumbled (75g),
- Sun-dried tomatoes: 1/4 cup, chopped (30g),
- Fresh parsley: 2tbsp, chopped(10g)
- Egg: 1 (50g),
- Breadcrumbs: 1/2 cup (60g),
- Salt and pepper: to taste

Instructions

- **Preparation:** Preheat the oven to 375ºF (190ºC). Chop onion, mince garlic, and chop sun-dried tomatoes.
- **Cooking:** Sauté onion and garlic in olive oil until soft. In a bowl, mix ground beef, ground lamb, sautéed onion and garlic, feta cheese, sun-dried tomatoes, parsley, egg, breadcrumbs, salt, and pepper. Shape mixture into a loaf and place in a baking dish. Bake for 1 hour until cooked through.
- **Assembly:** Ensure the meatloaf is evenly shaped and cooked.
- **Serving:** Serve hot, sliced, with a side of roasted vegetables or a fresh salad.

 Chef's Tips: "For a crispier crust, use more phyllo sheets."

 Calories: 400 kcal,
Carbohydrates: 30 g, Protein: 18 g, Fat: 24 g (Saturated Fat: 8 g, Monounsaturated Fat: 12 g, Polyunsaturated Fat: 2 g), Fiber: 5 g, Sugars: 6 g

 Interesting Fact: Spanakopita, a traditional Greek dish, is a savory pie filled with spinach, feta, and herbs, often enjoyed as a main dish or appetizer.

80 Seafood Risotto

Country of Origin: Italy

 Prep: 10 mins | **Cook:** 30 mins | **Total:** 40 mins | **Level:** 3/5 | **Servings:** 2

Ingredients

- Arborio rice: 1 cup (200g),
- Olive oil: 2 tbsp (30ml),
- Onion: 1, chopped (150g),
- Garlic: 2 cloves, minced (6g),
- Dry white wine: 1/2 cup (120ml),
- Vegetable broth: 4 cups (960ml),
- Mixed seafood (shrimp, scallops, mussels): 1 cup (200g),
- Parmesan cheese: 1/4 cup, grated (30g),
- Fresh parsley: 2 tbsp, chopped (10g),
- Lemon zest: 1 tsp (2g),
- Salt and pepper: to taste

Instructions

- **Preparation:** Chop onion and minced garlic.
- **Cooking:** Heat olive oil in a pan. Sauté onion and garlic until soft. Add Arborio rice, cook for 2min. Pour in white wine, stir until absorbed. Gradually add vegetable broth, one ladle at a time, stirring constantly until absorbed, about 20min. Add seafood, cook until just done, about 5min.
- **Assembly:** Stir in Parmesan, lemon zest, salt, and pepper.
- **Serving:** Serve hot, garnished with fresh parsley.

 Calories: 450 kcal, Carbohydrates: 55 g, Protein: 20 g, Fat: 15 g (Saturated Fat: 3 g, Monounsaturated Fat: 9 g, Polyunsaturated Fat: 2 g), Fiber: 3 g, Sugars: 5 g

 Interesting Fact: Risotto is a traditional Italian dish known for its creamy texture, often enhanced with fresh seafood in coastal regions.

 Chef's Tips: "For added flavor, use seafood broth instead of vegetable broth."

81 Mediterranean Baked Cod with Lemon and Garlic

Country of Origin: Mediterranean Region

 Prep: 10 mins | **Cook:** 20 mins | **Total:** 30 mins | **Level:** 2/5 | **Servings:** 2

Ingredients

- Cod fillets: 2 (300g),
- Olive oil: 2 tbsp (30ml),
- Lemon: 1, sliced (120g),
- Garlic: 3 cloves, minced (9g),
- Fresh parsley: 2 tbsp, chopped (10g),
- Salt and pepper: to taste,
- Cherry tomatoes: 1 cup, halved (150g)

Instructions

- **Preparation:** Preheat the oven to 375°F (190°C). Slice lemon and halve cherry tomatoes. Mince garlic.
- **Cooking:** Place cod fillets in a baking dish. Drizzle with olive oil, top with lemon slices, minced garlic, and cherry tomatoes. Season with salt and pepper. Bake for 20 min until cod is flaky and cooked through.
- **Assembly:** Ensure cod fillets are evenly coated with the olive oil mixture.
- **Serving:** Serve hot, garnished with fresh parsley.

 Chef's Tips: "For a more intense flavor, marinate the cod in the olive oil mixture for 15 minutes before baking."

 Calories: 350 kcal, Carbohydrates: 10 g, Protein: 35 g, Fat: 18 g (Saturated Fat: 3 g, Monounsaturated Fat: 10 g, Polyunsaturated Fat: 2 g), Fiber: 2 g, Sugars: 4 g

 Interesting Fact: Cod is a lean, protein-rich fish often used in Mediterranean cuisine for its mild flavor and versatility in various dishes.

MEDITERRANEAN SWEET INDULGENCES

Calories: 250 kcal,
Carbohydrates: 40 g, Protein: 4 g, Fat: 10 g (Saturated Fat: 6 g), Fiber: 1 g, Sugars: 30 g

Interesting Fact: Basbousa is a traditional Middle Eastern dessert, often enjoyed during festive occasions and celebrations.

Chef's Tips: "For a richer flavor, let the cake soak in the syrup overnight."

82 Basbousa (Semolina Cake)

Country of Origin: Middle East

Prep: 15 mins | **Cook:** 40 mins | **Total:** 55 mins | **Level:** 2/5 | **Servings:** 2

Ingredients

- Semolina: 2 cups (340g),
- Sugar: 1 cup (200g),
- Yogurt: 1 cup (240g),
- Butter: 1/2 cup, melted (120ml),
- Baking powder: 1 tsp (5g),
- Almonds: 12, blanched,
- Water: 1 1/2 cups (360ml),
- Lemon juice: 1 tbsp (15ml),
- Rose water: 1 tsp (5ml)

Instructions

- **Preparation:** Preheat oven to 350ºF (175ºC). Grease a baking dish.
- **Cooking:** Mix semolina, sugar, yogurt, melted butter, and baking powder. Pour into the baking dish. Score into diamond shapes, place an almond on each piece. Bake for 30-40 min until golden.
- **Assembly:** Make syrup by boiling water, sugar, and lemon juice for 10 min. Add rose water. Pour over hot cake.
- **Serving:** Let cool before serving.

83 Kataifi

 Country of Origin:
Turkey

 Prep: 30 mins | **Cook:** 30 mins | **Total:** 1 hr | **Level:** 4/5 | **Servings:** 2

Ingredients

- All-purpose flour: 1 cup (120g),
- Sugar: 1/4 cup (50g),
- Salt: 1/4 tsp (1.25g),
- Water: 1/2 cup (120ml),
- Butter: 1/2 cup, softened (120g),
- Ricotta cheese: 1/2 cup (125g),
- Semolina flour: 2 tbsp (30g),
- Milk: 1/2 cup (120ml),
- Egg: 1/2, beaten,
- Orange zest: 1/2 tsp (2.5g),
- Vanilla extract: 1/2 tsp (2.5ml),
- Powdered sugar: for dusting

Instructions

- **Preparation:** Mix flour, sugar, and salt. Gradually add water until dough forms. Knead until smooth. Wrap in plastic wrap and refrigerate for 30 min.
- **Cooking:** Boil milk, add semolina, and stir until thickened. Cool and mix with ricotta, egg, orange zest, and vanilla.
- **Assembly:** Roll dough thin, spread with softened butter, roll into log, and cut into 1-inch slices. Flatten slices, add filling, and fold to seal.
- **Baking:** Preheat oven to 375ºF (190ºC). Place on a baking sheet, brush with butter, and bake for 25-30 min until golden.
- **Serving:** Dust with powdered sugar.

84 Sfogliatelle

 Country of Origin:
Italy

 Prep: 20 mins | **Cook:** 30 mins | **Total:** 50 mins | **Level:** 4/5 | **Servings:** 2

Ingredients

- All-purpose flour: 1 cup (120g),
- Sugar: 1/4 cup (50g),
- Salt: 1/4 tsp (1.25g),
- Water: 1/2 cup (120ml),
- Butter: 1/2 cup, softened (120g),
- Ricotta cheese: 1/2 cup (125g),
- Semolina flour: 2 tbsp (30g),
- Milk: 1/2 cup (120ml),
- Egg: 1/2, beaten,
- Orange zest: 1/2 tsp (2.5g),
- Vanilla extract: 1/2 tsp (2.5ml),
- Powdered sugar: for dusting

Instructions

- **Preparation:** Mix flour, sugar, and salt. Add water until dough forms. Knead until smooth. Wrap and refrigerate for 30 min.
- **Cooking:** Boil milk, add semolina, and stir until thickened. Cool and mix with ricotta, egg, orange zest, and vanilla.
- **Assembly:** Roll dough thin, spread with butter, roll into log, and cut into 1-inch slices. Flatten slices, add filling, fold to seal.
- **Baking:** Preheat oven to 375ºF (190ºC). Place on a baking sheet, brush with butter, and bake for 25-30 min until golden.

 Calories: 350 kcal,
Carbohydrates: 40 g, Protein: 6 g, Fat: 18 g (Saturated Fat: 10 g), Fiber: 1 g, Sugars: 20 g

 Interesting Fact: Sfogliatelle, also known as "lobster tails," are a traditional Italian pastry known for their flaky layers and creamy filling.

 Chef's Tips: "Chill filled pastries before baking for extra crispiness."

 Chef's Tips: "Chill pastries before baking for extra crispiness."

 Calories: 350 kcal,
Carbohydrates: 40 g, Protein: 6 g, Fat: 18 g (Saturated Fat: 10 g), Fiber: 1 g, Sugars: 20 g

 Interesting Fact: Sfogliatelle, also known as "lobster tails," are a traditional Italian pastry known for their flaky layers and creamy filling.

 Loukoumades (Honey Puffs)

 Country of Origin: Greece

Prep: 15 mins | **Cook:** 30 mins | **Total:** 45 mins | **Level:** 2/5 | **Servings:** 3

Ingredients

- All-purpose flour: 1 cup (120g),
- Yeast: 1/2 tbsp (7.5g),
- Water: 3/4 cup (180ml),
- Sugar: 1/2 tbsp (7.5g),
- Salt: 1/4 tsp (1.25g),
- Honey: 1/4 cup (60ml),
- Cinnamon: 1/2 tsp (2.5g),
- Olive oil: for frying

Instructions

- **Preparation:** Dissolve yeast in warm water. Mix flour, sugar, and salt. Add yeast mixture, stir until smooth. Let rise for 1 hour.
- **Cooking:** Heat oil in a deep fryer. Drop batter by spoonfuls into hot oil, fry until golden. Drain on paper towels.
- **Assembly:** Drizzle with honey and sprinkle with cinnamon.
- **Serving:** Serve warm.

 Calories: 150 kcal, Carbohydrates: 25 g, Protein: 2 g, Fat: 5 g (Saturated Fat: 0.5 g), Fiber: 1 g, Sugars: 12 g

 Interesting Fact: Loukoumades are often enjoyed at Greek festivals and celebrations, known for their light and airy texture.

 Chef's Tips: "For an extra crunch, sprinkle with crushed nuts."

 Orange Almond Cake

 Country of Origin: Spain

Prep: 15 mins | **Cook:** 40 mins | **Total:** 55 mins | **Level:** 3/5 | **Servings:** 2

Ingredients

- Almond flour: 1 cup (120g),
- All-purpose flour: 1/2 cup (60g),
- Baking powder: 1 tsp (4g),
- Eggs: 3 (150g),
- Sugar: 1/2 cup (100g),
- Olive oil: 1/4 cup (60ml),
- Orange zest: 2 tbsp (6g),
- Orange juice: 1/4 cup (60ml),
- Vanilla extract: 1 tsp (5ml),
- Sliced almonds: 1/4 cup (30g)

Instructions

- **Preparation:** Preheat the oven to 350°F (175°C). Grease and flour a cake pan. Zest and juice the orange.
- **Cooking:** In a bowl, mix almond flour, all-purpose flour, and baking powder. In another bowl, beat eggs and sugar until fluffy. Add olive oil, orange zest, orange juice, and vanilla extract. Gradually fold in the flour mixture. Pour batter into the prepared pan and sprinkle with sliced almonds. Bake for 40 min until golden and a toothpick inserted comes out clean.
- **Assembly:** Ensure even distribution of batter and almonds.
- **Serving:** Let cool before slicing. Serve with a dusting of powdered sugar if desired.

 Chef's Tips: "For extra moisture, brush the warm cake with a syrup made from orange juice and sugar."

 Calories: 300 kcal, Carbohydrates: 35 g, Protein: 8 g, Fat: 15 g (Saturated Fat: 2 g, Monounsaturated Fat: 10 g, Polyunsaturated Fat: 2 g), Fiber: 4 g, Sugars: 20 g

 Interesting Fact: This traditional Spanish cake combines the bright flavors of orange with the nutty richness of almonds, making it a popular dessert in Mediterranean cuisine.

87 Lemon Olive Oil Cake

Country of Origin: Italy

 Prep: 15 mins | **Cook:** 45 mins | **Total:** 1 hr | **Level:** 3/5 | **Servings:** 2

Ingredients

- All-purpose flour: 1 cup (120g),
- Almond flour: 1/2 cup (60g),
- Baking powder: 1 tsp (4g),
- Eggs: 3 (150g),
- Sugar: 3/4 cup (150g),
- Olive oil: 1/2 cup (120ml),
- Lemon zest: 2 tbsp (6g),
- Lemon juice: 1/4 cup (60ml),
- Vanilla extract: 1 tsp (5ml),
- Powdered sugar: for dusting

Instructions

- **Preparation:** Preheat the oven to 350ºF (175ºC). Grease and flour a cake pan. Zest and juice the lemon.
- **Cooking:** In a bowl, mix all-purpose flour, almond flour, and baking powder. In another bowl, beat eggs and sugar until fluffy. Add olive oil, lemon zest, lemon juice, and vanilla extract. Gradually fold in the flour mixture. Pour batter into the prepared pan. Bake for 45 min until golden and a toothpick inserted comes out clean.
- **Assembly:** Ensure even distribution of batter.
- **Serving:** Let cool before slicing. Dust with powdered sugar before serving.

 Calories: 320 kcal, Carbohydrates: 35 g, Protein: 7 g, Fat: 18 g (Saturated Fat: 2.5 g, Monounsaturated Fat: 12 g, Polyunsaturated Fat: 2 g), Fiber: 2 g, Sugars: 25 g

 Interesting Fact: Lemon olive oil cake is a traditional Italian dessert that highlights the fresh flavors of lemon and the richness of olive oil, making it a perfect treat for any occasion.

 Chef's Tips: "For a moist cake, brush with a simple syrup made from lemon juice and sugar while still warm."

88 Galaktoboureko (Custard Pie)

Country of Origin: Greece

 Prep: 20 mins | **Cook:** 40 mins |  **Total:** 1 hr | **Level:** 3/5 | **Servings:** 6

Ingredients

- Phyllo dough: 1/2 package (8 oz),
- Butter: 1/2 cup, melted (120ml),
- Semolina: 1/2 cup (85g),
- Sugar: 1/2 cup (100g),
- Milk: 2 cups (480ml),
- Eggs: 2,
- Lemon zest: 1/2 tbsp (7.5g),
- Vanilla extract: 1/2 tsp (2.5ml),
- Water: 1/2 cup (120ml),
- Lemon juice: 1/2 tbsp (7.5ml)

Instructions

- **Preparation:** Preheat oven to 350ºF (175ºC). Grease a small baking dish.
- **Cooking:** Heat milk in a saucepan. Mix semolina, sugar, and lemon zest. Gradually add to milk, stirring constantly until thickened. Remove from heat, stir in eggs and vanilla. Layer phyllo sheets in the dish, brushing each with butter. Pour custard over phyllo. Top with remaining phyllo, brushing each with butter. Bake for 40 min until golden.
- **Assembly:** Boil sugar, water, and lemon juice for 10 min. Pour over hot galaktoboureko.

 Chef's Tips: "For a citrusy twist, add orange zest to the custard."

 Calories: 300 kcal, Carbohydrates: 40 g, Protein: 5 g, Fat: 15 g (Saturated Fat: 7 g), Fiber: 1 g, Sugars: 25 g

 Interesting Fact: Galaktoboureko is a traditional Greek dessert, loved for its creamy custard filling and crispy phyllo layers.

89 Pistachio Baklava

Country of Origin: Greece

Prep: 30 mins | **Cook:** 45 mins | **Total:** 1 hr 15 mins | **Level:** 4/5 | **Servings:** 2

Ingredients

- Phyllo dough: 8 sheets,
- Pistachios: 1 cup, chopped (120g),
- Butter: 1/2 cup, melted (120g),
- Sugar: 1/4 cup (50g),
- Honey: 1/4 cup (60ml),
- Water: 1/4 cup (60ml),
- Lemon juice: 1 tbsp (15ml),
- Cinnamon: 1 tsp (2g)

Instructions

- **Preparation:** Preheat the oven to 350°F (175°C). Chop pistachios and mix with cinnamon.
- **Cooking:** Layer 4 sheets of phyllo dough in a baking dish, brushing each with melted butter. Spread half of the pistachio mixture. Repeat with remaining phyllo and pistachio mixture. Cut into squares. Bake for 45 min until golden. In a saucepan, combine sugar, honey, water, and lemon juice. Bring to a boil, then simmer for 10 min.
- **Assembly:** Pour hot syrup over baklava immediately after baking.
- **Serving:** Let cool before serving.

Calories: 450 kcal,
Carbohydrates: 55 g, Protein: 6 g, Fat: 22 g (Saturated Fat: 10 g, Monounsaturated Fat: 8 g, Polyunsaturated Fat: 2 g), Fiber: 4 g, Sugars: 30 g

Interesting Fact: Baklava is a rich, sweet pastry made of layers of phyllo dough filled with chopped nuts and sweetened with syrup or honey, a beloved dessert in many Mediterranean cuisines.

Chef's Tips: "For best results, allow baklava to sit overnight to absorb the syrup."

90 Revani (Syrup-Soaked Cake)

Country of Origin: Greece, Turkey

Prep: 15 mins | **Cook:** 40 mins | **Total:** 55 mins | **Level:** 2/5 | **Servings:** 2

Ingredients

- Semolina: 1/2 cup (85g),
- All-purpose flour: 1/2 cup (60g),
- Sugar: 1/2 cup (100g),
- Yogurt: 1/2 cup (120g),
- Butter: 1/4 cup, melted (60ml),
- Eggs: 2,
- Baking powder: 1/2 tsp (2.5g),
- Lemon zest: 1/2 tbsp (7.5g),
- Water: 3/4 cup (180ml),
- Lemon juice: 1/2 tbsp (7.5ml),
- Rose water: 1/2 tsp (2.5ml)

Instructions

- **Preparation:** Preheat oven to 350°F (175°C). Grease a small baking dish.
- **Cooking:** Mix semolina, flour, sugar, yogurt, melted butter, eggs, baking powder, and lemon zest. Pour into the baking dish. Bake for 30-40 min until golden.
- **Assembly:** Boil water, sugar, lemon juice, and rose water for 10 min. Pour over hot cake.
- **Serving:** Let cool before serving.

Chef's Tips: "Serve with a dollop of whipped cream for added richness."

Calories: 250 kcal,
Carbohydrates: 40 g, Protein: 4 g, Fat: 10 g (Saturated Fat: 6 g), Fiber: 1 g, Sugars: 30 g

Interesting Fact: Revani is a moist and flavorful cake, traditionally enjoyed in Greece and Turkey, often served with tea or coffee.

91 Greek Yogurt with Honey and Nuts

 **Country of Origin:**
Greece

Prep: 5 mins | **Cook:** 0 mins | **Total:** 5 mins | **Level:** 1/5 | **Servings:** 1

Ingredients

- Greek yogurt: 1 cup (245g),
- Honey: 1 tbsp (21g),
- Chopped nuts (almonds, walnuts, or pistachios): 2 tbsp (30g)

Instructions

- **Preparation:** Spoon Greek yogurt into a bowl.
- **Assembly:** Drizzle honey over the yogurt. Sprinkle chopped nuts on top.
- **Serving:** Serve immediately, garnished with a sprig of mint or a few fresh berries for a pop of color, perhaps paired with a cup of herbal tea.

 Calories: 220 kcal,
Carbohydrates: 24 g, Protein: 10 g, Fat: 9 g (Saturated Fat: 2 g, Monounsaturated Fat: 3 g, Polyunsaturated Fat: 2 g), Cholesterol: 10 mg, Sodium: 70 mg, Fiber: 2 g, Sugars: 21 g

 Interesting Fact: Greek yogurt, known for its thick and creamy texture, has been a staple in Greek cuisine for centuries. It's often enjoyed with honey and nuts, a combination that dates back to ancient Greece.

 Chef's Tips: "Add a dash of cinnamon or a handful of fresh berries for extra flavor."

92 Amaretti Cookies

 Country of Origin:
Italy

Prep: 15 mins | **Cook:** 20 mins | **Total:** 35 mins | **Level:** 2/5 | **Servings:** 4

Ingredients

- Almond flour: 1 cup (100g),
- Sugar: 1/2 cup (100g),
- Egg whites: 2,
- Almond extract: 1/2 tsp (2.5ml),
- Powdered sugar: for dusting

Instructions

- **Preparation:** Preheat oven to 300ºF (150ºC). Line a baking sheet with parchment paper.
- **Cooking:** Beat egg whites until stiff peaks form. Fold in almond flour, sugar, and almond extract. Drop by spoonfuls onto the baking sheet. Dust with powdered sugar. Bake for 20 min until golden.
- **Assembly:** Let cool on a wire rack.
- **Serving:** Serve with coffee or tea.

 Chef's Tips: "For an extra refreshing twist, add a few slices of cucumber or a splash of sparkling water."

 Calories: 80 kcal,
Carbohydrates: 22 g, Protein: 0 g, Fat: 0 g (Saturated Fat: 0 g, Monounsaturated Fat: 0 g, Polyunsaturated Fat: 0 g), Fiber: 1 g, Sugars: 20 g

 Interesting Fact: Homemade lemonade is a classic Mediterranean drink known for its refreshing taste and simplicity.

93 Dried Fruit Compote

Country of Origin: Mediterranean Region

 Prep: 10 mins | **Cook:** 20 mins | **Total:** 30 mins | **Level:** 2/5 | **Servings:** 3

Ingredients

- Mixed dried fruits (e.g., apricots, figs, prunes): 1 cup (150g),
- Water: 2 cups (480ml),
- Sugar: 2 tbsp (25g),
- Lemon zest: 1 tsp (2g),
- Cinnamon stick: 1,
- Fresh mint leaves: for garnish

Instructions

- **Preparation:** Chop dried fruits into bite-sized pieces.
- **Cooking:** In a saucepan, combine dried fruits, water, sugar, lemon zest, and cinnamon stick. Bring to a boil, then reduce heat and simmer for 20 min until the fruits are tender and the liquid thickens.
- **Assembly:** Remove the cinnamon stick. Allow to cool slightly.
- **Serving:** Serve warm or chilled, garnished with fresh mint leaves.

 Calories: 180 kcal,
Carbohydrates: 45 g, Protein: 1 g, Fat: 0 g (Saturated Fat: 0 g, Monounsaturated Fat: 0 g, Polyunsaturated Fat: 0 g), Fiber: 5 g, Sugars: 40 g

 Interesting Fact: Dried fruit compote is a traditional Mediterranean dessert, enjoyed for its natural sweetness and the nutritional benefits of dried fruits, often served during festive occasions.

 Chef's Tips: "Add a splash of orange juice for extra citrus flavor."

94 Ricotta Cheesecake

Country of Origin: Italy

 Prep: 20 mins | **Cook:** 1 hr | **Total:** 1hr 20 mins | **Level:** 3/5 | **Servings:** 4

Ingredients

- Ricotta cheese: 1 cup (250g),
- Cream cheese: 1/2 cup (120g),
- Sugar: 1/2 cup (100g),
- Eggs: 2,
- Lemon zest: 1/2 tbsp (7.5g),
- Vanilla extract: 1/2 tsp (2.5ml),
- Graham cracker crust: 1 (6-inch)

Instructions

- **Preparation:** Preheat oven to 325ºF (165ºC). Prepare graham cracker crust in a small springform pan.
- **Cooking:** Beat ricotta, cream cheese, and sugar until smooth. Add eggs one at a time, beating well after each addition. Stir in lemon zest and vanilla. Pour into crust. Bake for 1 hour until set.
- **Assembly:** Cool in the pan before removing.
- **Serving:** Serve chilled, optionally with fresh berries.

 Chef's Tips: "For a smoother texture, use full-fat ricotta and cream cheese."

 Calories: 300 kcal,
Carbohydrates: 30 g, Protein: 10 g, Fat: 20 g (Saturated Fat: 12 g), Fiber: 0 g, Sugars: 25 g

 Interesting Fact: Ricotta cheesecake is a lighter variation of traditional cheesecake, featuring the mild and creamy flavor of ricotta cheese.

95 Panna Cotta

Country of Origin: Italy

Prep: 10 mins | **Cook:** 20 mins | **Total:** 20 mins + chilling | **Level:** 2/5 | **Servings:** 2

Ingredients

- Heavy cream: 1 cup (240ml),
- Sugar: 1/4 cup (50g),
- Gelatin: 1 tsp (5g),
- Vanilla extract: 1/2 tsp (2.5ml),
- Fresh berries: for garnish

Instructions

- **Preparation:** Dissolve gelatin in 1 tbsp of cold water. Set aside.
- **Cooking:** Heat cream and sugar in a saucepan over medium heat until sugar dissolves. Remove from heat, stir in gelatin and vanilla. Pour into ramekins.
- **Assembly:** Chill in the refrigerator for at least 4 hours until set.
- **Serving:** Unmold and garnish with fresh berries.

Calories: 350 kcal,
Carbohydrates: 25 g, Protein: 5 g, Fat: 30 g (Saturated Fat: 18 g), Fiber: 0 g, Sugars: 20 g

Interesting Fact: Panna cotta, meaning "cooked cream" in Italian, is a classic Italian dessert known for its silky smooth texture.

Chef's Tips: "For extra flavor, infuse the cream with vanilla beans."

96 Tiramisu

Country of Origin: Italy

Prep: 30 mins | **Cook:** 0 mins | **Total:** 30 mins + chilling | **Level:** 3/5 | **Servings:** 4

Ingredients

- Mascarpone cheese: 1 cup (250g),
- Heavy cream: 1/2 cup (120ml),
- Sugar: 1/4 cup (50g),
- Espresso: 1/2 cup (120ml),
- Ladyfingers: 12,
- Cocoa powder: for dusting,
- Coffee liqueur: 1 tbsp (15ml)

Instructions

- **Preparation:** Brew espresso, let cool. Whip cream and sugar until stiff peaks form. Fold in mascarpone.
- **Cooking:** Dip ladyfingers in espresso and coffee liqueur, layer in a dish. Spread mascarpone mixture over ladyfingers. Repeat layers.
- **Assembly:** Dust with cocoa powder.
- **Serving:** Chill for at least 4 hours before serving.

Chef's Tips: "For best results, chill overnight to allow flavors to meld."

Calories: 400 kcal,
Carbohydrates: 35 g, Protein: 6 g, Fat: 25 g (Saturated Fat: 15 g), Fiber: 1 g, Sugars: 20 g

Interesting Fact: Tiramisu, meaning "pick me up" in Italian, is a popular dessert made with layers of coffee-soaked ladyfingers and mascarpone cream.

97 Biscotti

Country of Origin: Italy

 Prep: 20 mins | **Cook:** 40 mins | **Total:** 1 hr | **Level:** 2/5 | **Servings:** 6

Ingredients

- All-purpose flour: 1 cup (120g),
- Sugar: 1/2 cup (100g),
- Baking powder: 1/2 tsp (2.5g),
- Salt: 1/8 tsp (0.5g),
- Eggs: 2,
- Almonds: 1/2 cup, chopped (75g),
- Vanilla extract: 1/2 tsp (2.5ml),
- Almond extract: 1/2 tsp (2.5ml)

Instructions

- **Preparation:** Preheat oven to 350ºF (175ºC). Line a baking sheet with parchment paper.
- **Cooking:** Mix flour, sugar, baking powder, and salt. Beat in eggs, vanilla, and almond extracts. Stir in almonds. Divide dough in half, shape into logs. Bake for 25 min. Cool slightly, slice, and bake for another 15 min until crisp.
- **Assembly:** Let cool on a wire rack.
- **Serving:** Serve with coffee or tea.

 Calories: 150 kcal,
Carbohydrates: 20 g, Protein: 3 g, Fat: 5 g (Saturated Fat: 1 g), Fiber: 1 g, Sugars: 12 g

 Interesting Fact: Biscotti, also known as cantucci, are Italian almond biscuits that are twice-baked and often enjoyed with a hot beverage.

 Chef's Tips: "AFor a chocolate twist, dip one end of each biscotti in melted chocolate."

98 Crostata (Italian Tart)

Country of Origin: Italy

 Prep: 20 mins | **Cook:** 40 mins | **Total:** 1hr | **Level:** 3/5 | **Servings:** 4

Ingredients

- All-purpose flour: 1 cup (120g),
- Sugar: 1/4 cup (50g),
- Butter: 1/2 cup, cold and diced (120g),
- Eggs: 1,
- Apricot jam: 1/2 cup (120g)

Instructions

- **Preparation:** Preheat oven to 350ºF (175ºC). Grease a small tart pan.
- **Cooking:** Mix flour and sugar. Cut in butter until crumbly. Add egg, mix until dough forms. Press dough into tart pan, spread jam over the top. Bake for 40 min until golden.
- **Assembly:** Let cool before slicing.
- **Serving:** Serve with a dollop of whipped cream.

 Chef's Tips: "Use any fruit jam or preserves you prefer."

 Calories: 300 kcal,
Carbohydrates: 40 g, Protein: 4 g, Fat: 15 g (Saturated Fat: 9 g), Fiber: 1 g, Sugars: 25 g

 Interesting Fact: Crostata is a rustic Italian tart filled with jam or fresh fruit, often enjoyed as a dessert or snack.

99 M'hanncha (Moroccan Snake Cake)

 Country of Origin: Morocco

 Prep: 30 mins | **Cook:** 40 mins | **Total:** 1 hr 10 mins | **Level:** 4/5 | **Servings:** 4

Ingredients

- Phyllo dough: 1/4 package (4 oz),
- Almond paste: 1 cup (250g),
- Sugar: 1/2 cup (100g),
- Butter: 1/4 cup, melted (60ml),
- Orange blossom water: 1/2 tbsp (7.5ml),
- Cinnamon: 1/2 tsp (2.5g),
- Almonds: 2 tbsp, chopped (20g),
- Honey: 1/4 cup (60ml)

Instructions

- **Preparation:** Preheat oven to 350ºF (175ºC). Grease a small baking dish.
- **Cooking:** Mix almond paste, sugar, orange blossom water, and cinnamon. Roll phyllo dough into a long snake-like shape, filling with almond mixture. Place in the dish, brush with butter. Bake for 40 min until golden.
- **Assembly:** Drizzle with honey and sprinkle with almonds.
- **Serving:** Let cool before serving.

 Calories: 400 kcal, Carbohydrates: 45 g, Protein: 8 g, Fat: 20 g (Saturated Fat: 8 g), Fiber: 4 g, Sugars: 35 g

 Interesting Fact: M'hanncha, meaning "snake" in Arabic, is a traditional Moroccan dessert made with phyllo dough and almond paste.

 Chef's Tips: "For a hint of sweetness, add a teaspoon of honey or agave syrup."

100 Honey & Almond Cookies

 **Country of Origin:** Mediterranean Region

 Prep: 15 mins | **Cook:** 20 mins | **Total:** 35 mins | **Level:** 2/5 | **Servings:** 6

Ingredients

- Almond flour: 1 cup (100g),
- Sugar: 1/4 cup (50g),
- Honey: 2 tbsp (30ml),
- Egg whites: 2,
- Almond extract: 1/2 tsp (2.5ml),
- Sliced almonds: 2 tbsp (20g),
- Powdered sugar: for dusting

Instructions

- **Preparation:** Preheat oven to 350ºF (175ºC). Line a baking sheet with parchment paper.
- **Cooking:** Beat egg whites until stiff peaks form. Fold in almond flour, sugar, honey, and almond extract. Drop by spoonfuls onto the baking sheet. Dust with powdered sugar. Bake for 20 min until golden.
- **Assembly:** Let cool on a wire rack.
- **Serving:** Serve with coffee or tea.

 Chef's Tips: "For a crunchy texture, add more sliced almonds on top before baking."

 Calories: 90 kcal, Carbohydrates: 12 g, Protein: 2 g, Fat: 4 g (Saturated Fat: 0.5 g), Fiber: 1 g, Sugars: 10 g

 Interesting Fact: Honey and almond cookies are a delightful Mediterranean treat, combining the rich flavors of honey and almonds in a light, crisp cookie.

Chapter 6: Meal Planning and Nutritional Insights for the Mediterranean Diet

Benefits of the Mediterranean Diet for Health

1. Heart and Vascular Health

The Mediterranean diet is rich in heart-healthy foods such as olive oil, nuts, and fish. These foods contain monounsaturated fats and omega-3 fatty acids, which help reduce the risk of heart disease by lowering bad cholesterol levels (LDL) and maintaining healthy blood pressure. Olive oil, a staple in this diet, is particularly beneficial due to its high content of oleic acid and polyphenols, which have been shown to improve endothelial function and reduce inflammation. Regular consumption of fatty fish like salmon and sardines provides essential omega-3 fatty acids, which are known to decrease triglyceride levels and improve overall cardiovascular health. Additionally, nuts such as almonds and walnuts contribute to a healthy lipid profile by increasing good cholesterol (HDL) and reducing oxidative stress.

2. Antioxidant Protection and Anti-Inflammatory Effects

The Mediterranean diet emphasizes fruits, vegetables, nuts, and whole grains, which are high in antioxidants like vitamins C and E, selenium, and carotenoids. These protect the body from oxidative stress and inflammation, reducing the risk of chronic diseases such as cancer and arthritis. The steady intake of phytonutrients from fruits and vegetables neutralizes free radicals and supports detoxification. Whole grains provide essential fiber for digestion and a healthy gut microbiome, while nuts and seeds, rich in vitamin E, protect cellular membranes and support immune function.

3. Weight Management

The Mediterranean diet promotes weight management with nutrient-dense, low-calorie foods. Focusing on whole foods, healthy fats, and fiber keeps you full, reducing overeating and aiding weight loss. It encourages eating a variety of vegetables, fruits, legumes, and whole grains for essential nutrients and sustained energy. Moderate intake of healthy fats from olive oil, nuts, and avocados ensures satisfying meals without excess calories. Lean proteins like fish, poultry, and plant-based options support muscle and metabolic health. The Mediterranean lifestyle also emphasizes regular physical activity and mindful eating, essential for long-term weight management and well-being.

The Mediterranean diet not only supports heart and vascular health, offers antioxidant protection, and aids in weight management, but it also ensures that everyone can enjoy delicious, diabetes-friendly meals, regardless of dietary restrictions.

To help you smoothly transition into this healthy lifestyle, the next chapter offers an introductory 4-week meal plan designed for a gentle start.

Chapter 7: An Inspiring 4-Week Meal Plan

Week 1: Meal Plan

W1	BREAKFAST	LUNCH	DINNER	SNACK
Sun	3. Avocado Toast with Poached Egg (p.11)	88. Galaktoboureko (Custard Pie) (p.55)	36. Vegetable and Cheese Lasagna (p.28)	62. Chicken Marsala (p.42)
Mon	5. Tomato and Spinach Omelette (p.12)	83. Kataifi (p.53)	25. Couscous with Vegetables and Spices (p.23)	51. Stewed Vegetables with Fish (p.36)
Tue	19. Protein Pancakes with Berries (p.19)	91. Greek Yogurt with Honey and Nuts (p.57)	27. Lemon Herb Salmon (p.23)	70. Greek Moussaka (p.46)
Wed	12. Yogurt with Granola and Berries (p.16)	96. Tiramisu (p.59)	34. Seafood Pasta (p.27)	73. Tabbouleh Salad with Fresh Herbs (p.47)
Thu	7. Eggs with Vegetables and Cheese (p.13)	84. Sfogliatelle (p.53)	40. Minestrone Soup(p.30)	75. Spinach and Feta Pie (p.48)
Fri	14. Yogurt Fruit Nut Salad (p.17)	86. Orange Almond Cake (p.54)	44. Lentil Stew with Vegetables (p.32)	65. Feta Stuffed Peppers (p.43)
Sat	16. Soft-Boiled Eggs with Greens (p.18)	97. Biscotti (p.60)	31. Chicken and Vegetable Casserole(p.26)	66. Lentil Soup with Spinach (p.44)

Week 2: Meal Plan

W2	BREAKFAST	LUNCH	DINNER	SNACK
Sun	1. Bruschetta (p.9)	89. Pistachio Baklava(p.56)	49. Baked Sea Bass with Herbs (p.35)	79. Mediterranean Meatloaf (p.50)
Mon	4. Blueberry Smoothie with Almonds (p.12)	82. Basbousa (Semolina Cake)(p.52)	28. Tuna and Bean Salad (p.24)	52. Vegetable Broth Soup (p.37)
Tue	13. Mushroom Spinach Omelette (p.16)	93. Dried Fruit Compote (p.58)	41. Grilled Fish with Vegetables (p.31)	74. Greek Chicken Gyros (p.48)
Wed	8. Banana Yogurt Pancakes (p.14)	83. Fruits with Nuts and Honey (p.52)	33. Turkey Meatballs with Tomato Sauce (p.27)	69. Vegetable Paella(p.45)
Thu	2. Oatmeal with Fruits and Seeds (p.10)	98. Crostata (Italian Tart) (p.60)	30. Garlic Shrimp with Parsley (p.25)	58. Grilled Lamb Chops with Herbs (p.40)
Fri	6. Oat Pancakes with Berries (p.13)	100. Honey and Almond Cookies (p.61)	24. Chicken Fillet with Tomatoes and Basil (p.21)	61. Shrimp and Vegetable Stir Fry (p.41)
Sat	10. Avocado and Tomato Toasts (p.15)	87. Lemon Olive Oil Cake (p.55)	48. Tuna with Tomatoes and Olives (p.34)	80. Seafood Risotto(p.51)

Week 3: Meal Plan

W3	BREAKFAST	LUNCH	DINNER	SNACK
Sun	9. Fruit Salad with Honey and Nuts (p.14)	85. Loukoumades (Honey Puffs) (p.54)	26. Stuffed Peppers with Rice and Vegetables (p.23)	54. Chickpea and Vegetable Stew (p.38)
Mon	15. Berry Smoothie(p.17)	91. Greek Yogurt with Honey and Nuts (p.57)	35. Stewed Meat with Vegetables (p.28)	76. Grilled Vegetable Skewers (p.49)
Tue	21. Shakshuka (p.20)	88. Galaktoboureko (Custard Pie) (p.55)	38. Chicken Spinach Cheese Rolls (p.29)	60. Saffron Rice with Vegetables (p.41)
Wed	20. Chia Seed Pudding with Mango (p.20)	99. M'hanncha (Moroccan Snake Cake) (p.61)	23. Grilled Fish with Lemon and Herbs (p.22)	55. Beef Stew with Vegetables (p.38)
Thu	16. Soft-Boiled Eggs with Greens (p.18)	84. Sfogliatelle (p.53)	42. Bean and Corn Salad (p.31)	68. Moroccan Chicken with Apricots (p.45)
Fri	14. Couscous with Vegetables and Hummus (p.17)	86. Orange Almond Cake (p.54)	39. Roasted Potatoes with Herbs (p.30)	71. Herbed Quinoa with Chickpeas (p.46)
Sat	18. Mediterranean Scrambled Eggs with Feta and Spinach (p.19)	95. Panna Cotta (p.59)	32. Whole Grain Pizza(p.26)	59. Ratatouille (p.40)

Week 4: Meal Plan

W4	BREAKFAST	LUNCH	DINNER	SNACK
Sun	5. Tomato and Spinach Omelette (p.12)	90. Revani (Syrup-Soaked Cake) (p.56)	46. Tomato Basil Soup(p.33)	67. Roasted Cauliflower with Tahini (p.44)
Mon	9. Fruit Salad with Honey and Nuts (p.14)	92. Amaretti Cookies (p.57)	50. Rosemary Lemon Chicken (p.35)	81. Mediterranean Baked Cod with Lemon and Garlic (p.51)
Tue	19. Protein Pancakes with Berries (p.19)	94. Ricotta Cheesecake (p.58)	37. Fish Cakes with Vegetables (p.29)	77. Stuffed Zucchini Boats (p.49)
Wed	3. Avocado Toast with Poached Egg (p.11)	84. Sfogliatelle (p.53)	43. Chicken Fillet withBroccoli and Lemon (p.31)	63. Pesto Pasta with Cherry Tomatoes (p.42)
Thu	12. Yogurt with Granola and Berries (p.16)	89. Pistachio Baklava(p.56)	49. Baked Sea Bass with Herbs (p.34)	78. Baked Eggplant with Tomatoes and Feta (p.50)
Fri	7. Eggs with Vegetables and Cheese (p.13)	97. Biscotti (p.60)	47. Buckwheat with Mushrooms and Vegetables (p.34)	72. Roasted Brussels Sprouts with Garlic(p.47)
Sat	4. Blueberry Smoothie with Almonds (p.12)	85. Baked Zucchini Chips (p.53)	22. Pasta with Vegetables and Olive Oil (p.21)	53. Baked Chicken with Potatoes and Herbs(p.36)

Chapter 8: Meal Planning Tips

Effective meal planning is essential for maintaining a balanced and healthy diet. It saves time, reduces food waste, and ensures you always have nutritious meals ready to go. This section provides practical tips for creating ready-to-use shopping lists and time-saving strategies in the kitchen.

Ready-to-Use Shopping Lists

1. Categorize Your List:

- **Produce:** Spinach, tomatoes, avocados, blueberries, bananas, lemons, carrots, bell peppers
- **Dairy:** Greek yogurt, eggs, milk, cheese
- **Meat & Seafood:** Chicken breasts, salmon fillets, ground turkey, tuna
- Pantry Items: Quinoa, couscous, whole grain bread, olive oil, honey, nuts, seeds, canned beans
- **Frozen:** Mixed vegetables, fruit for smoothies
- **Spices & Condiments:** Salt, pepper, basil, oregano, cumin, paprika

2. Check Your Pantry First:

- Before you make your shopping list, check your pantry, fridge, and freezer to see what you already have. This helps avoid buying duplicates and reduces waste.

3. Plan for Freshness:

- Buy fresh produce in smaller quantities to use within the first few days of the week. Opt for frozen or longer-lasting items for meals later in the week.

4. Include Staples:

- Ensure you always have staple items on hand like olive oil, spices, and grains that you'll use frequently.

Time-Saving Tips in the Kitchen

1. Prep Ahead:

- Spend time on the weekend or during free periods chopping vegetables, marinating meats, and preparing grains. Store them in the fridge or freezer for easy access during the week.

2. Use Kitchen Gadgets:

- Utilize tools like slow cookers, pressure cookers, and food processors to cut down on cooking and prep time. These gadgets can help you prepare meals with minimal hands-on time.

3. Batch Cooking:

- Cook large quantities of staple items like grains, beans, and proteins that can be used in multiple meals throughout the week. This is particularly useful for items like rice, quinoa, and grilled chicken.

4. Clean As You Go:

- Keep your workspace tidy by cleaning up as you cook. This will save time on post-meal cleanup and make the cooking process more enjoyable.

5. Organize Your Kitchen:

- Keep frequently used items within easy reach and maintain an organized pantry and fridge so you can quickly find what you need. Labeling containers and shelves can also save time.

⭐ **Additional Tips:**

- *When cooking, consider doubling recipes and freezing half for future meals.*
- *Opt for one-pot meals that reduce the number of dishes and streamline the cooking process.*
- *Prepare healthy snacks like cut-up vegetables, fruit, and nuts ahead of time so they're ready to grab and go.*

BONUS 1: Ready-to-Use Shopping Lists

These shopping lists provide an approximate guide to the essential ingredients for the meals planned each week. Please adjust the quantities according to the number of servings and individual preferences. Before heading to the store, check your pantry to see what you already have at home to avoid unnecessary duplicates.

Example Shopping List for the Week 1:

Produce:	Nuts & Seeds:
• Spinach: 4 cups (2 bags), • Tomatoes: 12, • Avocados: 2, • Blueberries: 1 pint (500g), • Lemons: 4, Carrots: 1 bag (500g), • Bell peppers: 6, • Fresh herbs (parsley, dill, mint, basil): 1 bunch each, • Garlic: 2 heads, • Zucchini: 3, • Cucumbers: 2, • Eggplant: 2, • Oranges: 4, • Mixed vegetables (for lasagna, casserole, and soups)	• Mixed nuts: 1 bag (500g), • Almonds: 1 bag (500g), • Chia seeds: 1 bag (200g), • Walnuts: 1 bag (500g)

Dairy:	Spices & Condiments:
• Greek yogurt: 1 quart (946ml), • Eggs: 2 dozen, • Feta cheese: 2 cups (450g), • Shredded cheese: 2 cups (200g), • Milk or plant-based milk: 1 gallon (3.8L), • Parmesan cheese: 1 cup (100g), • Ricotta cheese: 1 cup (250g), • Plain yogurt (for snacks): 1 pint (500g)	• Olive oil: 1 bottle (500ml), • Honey: 1 jar (340g), • Salt, • Black pepper, • Dried oregano, • Dried basil, • Cinnamon, • Red pepper flakes, • Balsamic vinegar: 1 bottle (500ml), • Vanilla extract (for desserts)

Meat & Seafood:	Frozen:
• Chicken breasts: 4 (1.5 lbs / 680g), • Fish fillets (for various recipes): 4 (1.5 lbs / 680g), • Mixed seafood: 1 lb (450g), • Salmon fillets: 2 (1 lb / 450g), • Ground beef: 1 lb (450g)	• Mixed vegetables: 2 bags (1kg), • Mixed fruit for smoothies: 1 bag (500g)

Grains & Legumes:	Beverages:
• Whole grain bread: 1 loaf (500g), • Couscous: 1 box (500g), • Whole grain pasta: 1 box (500g), • Lasagna noodles: 1 box (500g), • Quinoa: 1 bag (500g), • Lentils: 1 bag (500g), • Whole grain flour: 1 bag (1kg)	• Herbal tea (mint, chamomile), • Orange juice (1L), • Pomegranate juice (1L)

Example Shopping List for the Week 2:

Produce:	Nuts & Seeds:
• Spinach: 3 cups (1.5 bags), • Tomatoes: 14, • Avocados: 3, • Blueberries: 1 pint (500g), • Bananas: 3 (for pancakes), • Lemons: 4, • Carrots: 1 bag (500g), • Bell peppers: 8, • Fresh herbs (parsley, dill, mint, basil): 1 bunch each, • Garlic: 2 heads, • Zucchini: 3, • Cucumbers: 2, • Eggplant: 1, • Oranges: 4, • Mixed vegetables (for soups, stir fry, and paella)	• Mixed nuts: 1 bag (500g), • Almonds: 1 bag (500g), • Chia seeds: 1 bag (200g), • Walnuts: 1 bag (500g), • Pistachios: 1 bag (500g, for baklava)

Dairy:	Spices & Condiments:
• Greek yogurt: 1 quart (946ml), • Eggs: 2 dozen, • Feta cheese: 2 cups (450g), • Shredded cheese: 2 cups (200g), • Milk or plant-based milk: 1 gallon (3.8L), • Parmesan cheese: 1 cup (100g), • Ricotta cheese: 1 cup (250g, for crostata), • Plain yogurt (for snacks): 1 pint (500g)	• Olive oil: 1 bottle (500ml), • Honey: 1 jar (340g), • Salt, • Black pepper, • Dried oregano, • Dried basil, • Cinnamon, • Red pepper flakes, • Balsamic vinegar: 1 bottle (500ml), • Vanilla extract (for desserts)

Meat & Seafood:	Frozen:
• Chicken breasts: 4 (1.5lbs / 680g), • Tuna: 4 fillets (1.5 lbs / 680g), • Sea bass: 2 (1.5 lbs / 680g), • Mixed seafood: 1 lb (450g, for risotto), • Shrimp: 2 lbs (900g), • Ground beef: 1 lb (450g), • Lamb chops: 4 (1 lb / 450g), • Turkey: 1 lb (450g), • Chicken fillets: 2 (1 lb / 450g)	• Mixed vegetables: 2 bags (1kg), • Mixed fruit for smoothies: 1 bag (500g)

Grains & Legumes:	Beverages:
• Whole grain bread: 1 loaf (500g, for bruschetta), • Couscous: 1 box (500g), • Whole grain pasta: 1 box (500g), • Lasagna noodles: 1 box (500g), • Quinoa: 1 bag (500g), • Lentils: 1 bag (500g), • Whole grain flour: 1 bag (1kg), • Rice: 1 bag (500g, for paella and risotto), • Oats: 1 bag (500g)	• Herbal tea (mint, chamomile), • Orange juice (1L), • Pomegranate juice (1L)

Example Shopping List for the Week 3:

Produce:

- Spinach: 3 cups (1.5 bags, for breakfast and rolls),
- Tomatoes: 10 (for shakshuka and salad),
- Avocados: 1,
- Blueberries: 1 pint (500g, for smoothie),
- Bananas: 3,
- Lemons: 4 (for fish and skewers),
- Carrots: 1 bag (500g, for stew),
- Bell peppers: 6 (for stuffed peppers and skewers),
- Fresh herbs (parsley, dill, mint, basil): 1 bunch each,
- Garlic: 2 heads (for various dishes),
- Zucchini: 3 (for skewers),
- Cucumbers: 2 (for salad),
- Eggplant: 1,
- Oranges: 4,
- Mixed vegetables (for stews, skewers, and ratatouille),
- Mango: 1 (for chia seed pudding),
- Apricots: 1 bag (for Moroccan chicken)

Nuts & Seeds:

- Mixed nuts: 1 bag (500g, for snacks),
- Almonds: 1 bag (500g),
- Chia seeds: 1 bag (200g, for pudding),
- Walnuts: 1 bag (500g),
- Pistachios: 1 bag (500g, for baklava),
- Sesame seeds: 1 bag (100g)

Spices & Condiments:

- Olive oil: 1 bottle (500ml),
- Honey: 1 jar (340g, for snacks and desserts),
- Salt,
- Black pepper,
- Dried oregano,
- Dried basil,
- Cinnamon,
- Red pepper flakes,
- Balsamic vinegar: 1 bottle (500ml),
- Vanilla extract (for desserts),
- Saffron: 1 bag (for rice),
- Turmeric: 1 bag (for Moroccan chicken),
- Cumin: 1 bag,
- Paprika: 1 bag,
- Baking powder: 1 bag (for baking),
- Semolina: 1 bag (for basbousa),
- Dried fruits: 1 bag (for compote),
- Baklava syrup

Dairy:

- Greek yogurt: 1 quart (946ml, for snacks and smoothies),
- Eggs: 2 dozen (for breakfasts and baking),
- Feta cheese: 2 cups (450g),
- Shredded cheese: 2 cups (200g, for pizza),
- Milk or plant-based milk: 1 gallon (3.8L),
- Parmesan cheese: 1 cup (100g),
- Ricotta cheese: 1 cup (250g, for sfogliatelle),
- Plain yogurt (for snacks): 1 pint (500g),
- Cheese (for rolls): 1 cup (250g)

Frozen:

- Mixed vegetables: 2 bags (1kg, for stir fry and various dishes),
- Mixed fruit for smoothies: 1 bag (500g, for smoothie)

Beverages:

- Herbal tea (mint, chamomile),
- Orange juice (1L, for snacks),
- Pomegranate juice (1L, for snacks)

Meat & Seafood:

- Chicken breasts: 4 (1.5 lbs / 680g, for rolls and Moroccan chicken),
- Tuna: 2 fillets (1 lb / 450g),
- Mixed seafood: 1 lb (450g),
- Shrimp: 1 lb (450g),
- Ground beef: 1 lb (450g, for stew),
- Lamb chops: 2 (1 lb / 450g),
- Turkey: 1 lb (450g),
- Chicken fillets: 2 (1 lb / 450g),
- Beef: 1 lb (450g, for stew)

Grains & Legumes:

- Whole grain bread: 1 loaf (500g, for pizza),
- Couscous: 1 box (500g, for salad),
- Whole grain pasta: 1 box (500g, for various dishes),
- Lasagna noodles: 1 box (500g),
- Quinoa: 1 bag (500g, for quinoa with chickpeas),
- Lentils: 1 bag (500g, for stew),
- Whole grain flour: 1 bag (1kg, for baking),
- Rice: 1 bag (500g, for saffron rice),
- Oats: 1 bag (500g),
- Beans: 1 can (for salad),
- Corn: 1 can (for salad),
- Chickpeas: 2 cans (for hummus and stew)

Example Shopping List for the Week 4:

Produce:

- Spinach: 4 cups (2 bags),
- Tomatoes: 12,
- Avocados: 2,
- Blueberries: 1 pint (500g),
  Bananas: 3,
- Lemons: 6,
- Carrots: 1 bag (500g),
- Bell peppers: 6,
- Fresh herbs (parsley, dill, mint, basil, rosemary): 1 bunch each,
- Garlic: 2 heads,
- Zucchini: 4 (for stuffed zucchini boats and baked zucchini chips),
- Cucumbers: 2,
- Eggplant: 2 (for baked eggplant),
- Broccoli: 1 head,
- Brussels sprouts: 1 bag (500g),
- Cauliflower: 1 head,
- erries (for yogurt and pancakes),
- Cherry tomatoes: 1 pint (500g)

Nuts & Seeds:

- Mixed nuts: 1 bag (500g, for snacks),
- Almonds: 1 bag (500g),
- Chia seeds: 1 bag (200g, for pudding),
- Walnuts: 1 bag (500g),
- Pistachios: 1 bag (500g, for baklava),
- Sesame seeds: 1 bag (100g)

Dairy:

- Greek yogurt: 1 quart (946ml),
- Eggs: 2 dozen,
- Feta cheese: 2 cups (450g),
- Shredded cheese: 2 cups (200g),
- Milk or plant-based milk: 1 gallon (3.8L),
- Parmesan cheese: 1 cup (100g),
- Ricotta cheese: 1 cup (250g, for cheesecake),
- Plain yogurt (for snacks): 1 pint (500g)

Spices & Condiments:

- Olive oil: 1 bottle (500ml),
- Honey: 1 jar (340g, for snacks and desserts),
- Salt,
- Black pepper,
- Dried oregano,
- Dried basil,
- Cinnamon,
- Red pepper flakes,
- Balsamic vinegar: 1 bottle (500ml),
- Vanilla extract (for desserts),
- Saffron: 1 bag (for rice),
- Turmeric: 1 bag (for Moroccan chicken),
- Cumin: 1 bag, Paprika: 1 bag,
- Baking powder: 1 bag (for baking),
- Semolina: 1 bag (for basbousa),
- Dried fruits: 1 bag (for compote),
- Baklava syrup

Meat & Seafood:

- Chicken breasts: 6 (2 lbs / 900g),
- Cod: 2 fillets (1 lb / 450g),
- Sea bass: 2 (1.5 lbs / 680g),
- Ground beef: 1 lb (450g, for meatballs),
- Salmon fillets: 2 (1 lb / 450g),
- Mixed seafood: 1 lb (450g, for risotto),
- Shrimp: 1 lb (450g),
- Ground turkey: 1 lb (450g, for stuffed zucchini boats),
- Beef: 1 lb (450g, for stew)

Frozen:

- Mixed vegetables: 2 bags (1kg, for stir fry and various dishes),
- Mixed fruit for smoothies: 1 bag (500g, for smoothie)

Beverages:

- Herbal tea (mint, chamomile),
- Orange juice (1L, for snacks),
- Pomegranate juice (1L, for snacks)

Grains & Legumes:

- Whole grain bread: 1 loaf (500g, for bruschetta),
- Couscous: 1 box (500g),
- Whole grain pasta: 1 box (500g),
- Lasagna noodles: 1 box (500g),
- Quinoa: 1 bag (500g), Lentils: 1 bag (500g),
- Whole grain flour: 1 bag (1kg),
- Rice: 1 bag (500g, for saffron rice),
- Oats: 1 bag (500g), Beans: 1 can (for salad),
- Corn: 1 can (for salad),
- Chickpeas: 2 cans (for hummus and stew),
- Buckwheat: 1 bag (500g, for buckwheat with mushrooms)

BONUS 2:   Adapting the 4-week Meal Plan to Different Lifestyles

To further personalize the unified 4-week meal plan, here are specific adaptations for each target group based on their unique needs and preferences. This section provides practical tips on how to make the meal plan work best for: **Busy Professionals, Families with Children,** individuals with **an Active Lifestyle,** and **Seniors.**

FOR BUSY PROFESSIONALS:	
Batch Cooking:	Prepare large portions of meals like stews (e.g., 35. Stewed Meat with Vegetables) and casseroles (e.g., 31. Chicken and Vegetable Casserole) on weekends, then portion them out for the week.
Grab-and-Go Breakfasts:	Focus on recipes like smoothies (e.g., 4. Blueberry Smoothie with Almonds), overnight oats, and yogurt parfaits (e.g., 1. Greek Yogurt with Honey and Nuts) that can be quickly assembled or made ahead.
Portable Snacks:	Keep nuts, fruits, and homemade energy bars handy for quick snacks during work hours.
Simple Lunches:	Opt for easy-to-pack lunches such as grain salads (e.g., 28. Tuna and Bean Salad), wraps, (e.g., 74. Greek Chicken Gyros) and sandwiches.

★ **Adaptation Tips:**

- *Batch cook lunches and dinners that can be reheated.*
- *Select breakfast recipes that require minimal preparation, like smoothies or yogurt with granola.*
- *Keep a variety of snacks like nuts, fruit, and homemade energy bars on hand for quick energy boosts.*

Interactive Meals:	Choose recipes that allow children to participate in the cooking process, such as making their own pizzas (e.g., 32. Whole Grain Pizza) or assembling salads(e.g., 27. Bean and Corn Salad).

Colorful Dishes:	Use a variety of colorful vegetables and fruits to make meals visually appealing and fun for children (e.g., 19. Protein Pancakes with Berries).

Healthy Snacks:	Prepare kid-friendly snacks like fruit salads (e.g. 9. Fruit Salad with Honey and Nuts), veggie sticks (e.g., 76. Grilled Vegetable Skewers), and healthy fruits and nuts (e.g., 93. Dried Fruit Compote).

Family-Style Meals:	Plan dinners that can be served family-style, encouraging everyone to eat together and try different dishes (e.g., 40. Minestrone Soup or 63. Pesto Pasta with Cherry Tomatoes).

★ **Adaptation Tips:**

- *Incorporate colorful and fun foods that kids are more likely to enjoy.*
- *Involve children in meal preparation to make them more interested in eating healthy.*
- *Plan for leftovers that can be used in different ways to reduce food waste and save time.*

FOR AN ACTIVE LIFESTYLE:

High-Protein Options:	Add extra protein sources such as grilled chicken, fish, or legumes to meals (e.g., 27. Lemon Herb Salmon or 41. Grilled Fish with Vegetables).
Carb Timing:	Schedule high-carb meals around workout times to optimize energy and recovery (e.g.,2. Oatmeal with Fruits and Seeds).
Hydration Focus:	Include beverages like water, herbal teas, and electrolyte drinks to stay hydrated throughout the day.
Pre- and Post-Workout Snacks:	Incorporate snacks that provide quick energy before workouts and aid recovery afterward, such as fruit with nuts or a smoothie (e.g., 11. Green Fruit Smoothie).

★ **Adaptation Tips:**

- *Add extra protein sources like chicken, fish, or beans to meals.*
- *Schedule high-carb meals around workout times for maximum energy.*
- *Keep hydration options like water and herbal teas readily available.*

FOR SENIORS:

Soft Foods:	Select recipes that include softer foods that are easier to chew and digest, like soups (e.g., 46. Tomato Basil Soup), stews (e.g., 29. Stewed Vegetables with Chicken), and soft foods (e.g., 16. Soft-Boiled Eggs with Greens)

★ **Adaptation Tips:**

- *Select softer foods that are easier to chew and digest.*
- *Incorporate dairy or fortified alternatives to boost calcium intake.*
- *Plan for smaller, more frequent meals to maintain energy levels.*

Example Adaptations for Specific Recipes:

91. GREEK YOGURT WITH HONEY AND NUTS

Busy Professionals:	Prepare individual servings in mason jars for a quick grab-and-go breakfast.
Families with Children:	Add a variety of toppings such as berries, granola, and seeds to make it fun for kids to customize their own bowls.
Active Lifestyle:	Add a scoop of protein powder or a handful of nuts to increase protein content.
Seniors:	Choose plain Greek yogurt for less sugar and add honey sparingly for sweetness.

23. GRILLED FISH WITH LEMON AND HERBS

Busy Professionals:	Prepare extra fillets and store them in the fridge for easy reheating throughout the week.
Families with Children:	Serve with a side of colorful vegetables or a fun-shaped pasta to make the meal more appealing to kids.
Active Lifestyle:	Pair with a quinoa or brown rice salad to provide a balanced meal with protein and carbs.
Seniors:	Opt for a softer fish like salmon and ensure it is cooked to a tender consistency.

24. CHICKEN FILLET WITH TOMATOES AND BASIL

Busy Professionals:	Slice the chicken fillets and add them to salads or wraps for quick lunches.
Families with Children:	Serve with a side of mashed potatoes or rice to make it a complete, kid-friendly meal.
Active Lifestyle:	Add a side of roasted sweet potatoes for extra carbohydrates.
Seniors:	Ensure the chicken is tender and easy to chew, perhaps cooking it in a slow cooker for extra softness.

This flexible approach ensures that the meal plan can meet the diverse needs of various lifestyles while adhering to the principles of the Mediterranean diet.

BONUS 3: Frequently Asked Questions

Maintaining the Mediterranean diet involves planning meals, staying consistent, and enjoying a variety of foods within the diet's guidelines.

Here are some questions people often ask about the Mediterranean diet.

QUESTION	ANSWER
What exactly do you eat on a Mediterranean diet?	There is no single Mediterranean diet. Rather, it is an approach that focuses on fresh, unprocessed foods, a variety of fruits and vegetables, and whole foods. Seafood, fish, dairy products, and legumes provide protein, along with some meat.
What do I eat on the Mediterranean diet to lose weight?	Overall caloric intake and energy expenditure are more important for weight loss than any specific diet composition. However, the Mediterranean diet contains healthy carbohydrates, fats, and other nutrients. Prioritizing whole vegetables and grains may help people lose weight as part of an overall calorie deficit.
Is the Mediterranean diet anti-inflammatory?	Eating a Mediterranean diet may have an anti-inflammatory effect compared to other Western diets. However, research is ongoing to fully understand the mechanisms of this effect.
What are the 9 components of the Mediterranean diet?	The Mediterranean diet encompasses a wide range of foods and drinks. However, it emphasizes: 1. **vegetables** 2. **healthy oils, like olive oil** 3. **whole grains** 4. **legumes** 5. **fruits and nuts** 6. **fish and shellfish** 7. **low fat dairy** 8. **lean proteins** 9. **moderate alcohol intake**

QUESTION	ANSWER
How do I start and maintain the Mediterranean diet?	Starting and maintaining the Mediterranean diet involves gradual changes and consistency. Here are steps to get you started: 1. **Incorporate More Fruits and Vegetables:** Aim to fill half your plate with fruits and vegetables at every meal. 2. **Choose Whole Grains:** Replace refined grains with whole grains like quinoa, brown rice, and whole wheat bread. 3. **Opt for Healthy Fats:** Use olive oil instead of butter. Include avocados, nuts, and seeds in your diet. 4. **Eat More Seafood:** Include fish or seafood in your meals at least twice a week. 5. **Limit Red Meat:** Replace red meat with poultry, fish, and plant-based proteins like beans and legumes. 6. **Enjoy Dairy in Moderation:** Choose low-fat or fat-free dairy options and consume in moderate amounts. 7. **Use Herbs and Spices:** Enhance flavors with herbs and spices instead of salt. 8. **Stay Active:** Complement your diet with regular physical activity.
How can I adapt recipes for common food allergies?	Adapting recipes for food allergies involves substituting allergens with safe alternatives. Here are some common substitutions: 1. **Dairy Allergy**: Use plant-based milks (almond, soy, coconut) instead of cow's milk. Replace butter with margarine or coconut oil. For cheese, try dairy-free options made from nuts or soy. 2. **Gluten Allergy**: Use gluten-free grains like quinoa, rice, or gluten-free pasta instead of wheat-based products. Replace flour with gluten-free flour blends. 3. **Nut Allergy**: Substitute nuts with seeds (sunflower, pumpkin) or nut-free spreads. 4. **Egg Allergy**: Use applesauce, mashed banana, or commercial egg replacers as a binding agent in baking. 5. **Soy Allergy**: Substitute soy sauce with coconut aminos or tamari (check for gluten- free). 6. **Seafood Allergy**: Use chicken, tofu, or legumes as protein alternatives in seafood dishes.

BONUS 4: Quick Fixes

Practically everyone has experienced that dreadful moment in the kitchen when a recipe fails just as dinner guests arrive. These handy tips can save the day!

Acidic foods	If a tomato-based sauce becomes too acidic, add baking soda, one teaspoon at a time. You can also use sugar as a sweeter alternative.
Burnt food on pots and pans	Allow the pan to cool on its own. Remove as much food as possible. Fill with hot water and add a capful of liquid fabric softener; let it stand for a few hours. This will make it easier to remove the burnt food.
Chocolate seizes	Chocolate can seize (turn coarse and grainy) when it comes into contact with water. Place seized chocolate in a metal bowl over a saucepan with an inch of simmering water. Over medium heat, slowly whisk in warm heavy cream (use 1/4 cup cream for 4 ounces of chocolate). The chocolate will melt and become smooth.
Forgot to thaw whipped topping	Thaw in the microwave for 1 minute on the defrost setting. Stir to blend well. Avoid over-thawing!
Hands smell like garlic or onion	Rinse hands under cold water while rubbing them with a large stainless steel spoon.
Lumpy gravy or sauce	Use a blender, food processor, or simply strain to remove lumps.
Hard brown sugar	Place in a paper bag and microwave for a few seconds, or put hard chunks in a food processor.
No tomato juice	Mix 1/2 cup ketchup with 1/2 cup water as a substitute.
Out of honey	Substitute 1 1/4 cups sugar dissolved in 1 cup water.
Overcooked sweet potatoes or carrots	Use softened sweet potatoes and carrots to make a soufflé with the addition of eggs and sugar. Consult your favorite cookbook for a soufflé recipe. Overcooked sweet potatoes can also be used as pie filling.
Sandwich bread is stale	Toast or microwave bread briefly. Alternatively, turn it into breadcrumbs. Bread exposed to light and heat will spoil faster, so consider using a bread box.
Soup, sauce, or gravy too thin	Add 1 tablespoon of flour to hot soup, sauce, or gravy. Whisk well to avoid lumps while the mixture is boiling. Repeat if necessary.
Sticky rice	Rinse rice with warm water.
Stew or soup is greasy	Refrigerate and remove grease once it congeals. Another trick is to lay cold lettuce leaves over the hot stew for about 10 seconds and then remove. Repeat as necessary.
Too salty	Add a small amount of sugar or vinegar. In soups or sauces, add a raw, peeled potato to absorb the salt.
Too sweet	Add a little vinegar or lemon juice to balance the sweetness.

BONUS 5: Table Settings

LUNCHEON TABLE SETTING

1. Bread and butter plate and knife
2. Water glass
3. Optional drink glass
4. Napkin
5. Luncheon fork
6. Dessert fork
7. First course bowl and liner plate
8. Luncheon plate
9. Knife
10. Teaspoon
11. Soup spoon

DINNER TABLE SETTING

1. Salad plate
2. Water glass
3. Optional drink glass
4. Napkin
5. Salad fork
6. Dinner fork
7. Dessert fork
8. First course bowl and liner plate
9. Dinner plate
10. Dinner knife
11. Teaspoon
12. Soup spoon

Index

Conclusion

Adopting the Mediterranean diet is more than just changing your eating habits; it's a lifestyle that embraces wholesome, delicious food, physical activity, and meaningful connections. By following the recipes and tips in this book, you are taking an important step towards a healthier, more vibrant life.

Embark on your Mediterranean diet journey with enthusiasm and curiosity. Create a lifestyle that nourishes your body and brings joy to your everyday life. Enjoy meals with loved ones, explore new recipes, and savor the rich culinary heritage of the Mediterranean.
We hope this cookbook has inspired you to make lasting changes for your overall well-being. Remember, the journey to health is a continuous process, and every small step brings you closer to your goals.

Bon Appétit and Best Wishes!
Sincerely, Moira Boyd

Notes: